P9-DGL-029

Towns and Villages
OF ENGLAND

CHIPPING CAMPDEN

Shepherd Hedges, who lived at Paul's Pike, *c.* 1904–5.   CADHAS

Towns and Villages
OF ENGLAND

CHIPPING CAMPDEN

CATHERINE GORDON

ALAN SUTTON

First published in the United Kingdom in 1993 by
Alan Sutton Publishing Ltd · Phoenix Mill · Far Thrupp · Stroud
Gloucestershire

First published in the United States of America in 1993 by
Alan Sutton Publishing Inc. · 83 Washington Street · Dover · NH 03820

Copyright © Catherine Gordon, 1993

All rights reserved. No part of this publication may be reproduced, stored in a
retrieval system, or transmitted, in any form, or by any means, electronic,
mechanical, photocopying, recording or otherwise, without the prior
permission of the publishers and copyright holder.

British Library Cataloguing in Publication Data

A record for this book is available from the British Library

ISBN 0-7509-0492-5

Library of Congress Cataloging in Publication Data applied for

Cover illustrations: front: The sheep market in the Market Square, c. 1910
(Campden Trust); back: the High Street (Campden Trust)

Typeset in 11/13 Bembo.
Typesetting and origination by
Alan Sutton Publishing Limited.
Printed in Great Britain by
Hartnolls Ltd, Bodmin, Cornwall.

Contents

Acknowledgements   vi

Introduction   vii

Chapter One: The Gift of the Golden Fleece   1

Chapter Two: The New Rule   14

Chapter Three: C.R. Ashbee and the Guild of Handicraft   30

Chapter Four: The City of the Sun   48

Chapter Five: Rebuilding Utopia   63

Chapter Six: The Legacy of the Guild   72

Chapter Seven: The Conservation of Campden   80

Bibliography   87

Index   88

Acknowledgements

Writing this book has provided me with an excellent excuse to spend plenty of time in Chipping Campden, where I have constantly met with a friendly welcome from both residents and shopkeepers. In particular, I would like to thank Mr and Mrs John Williams of Dover's Court, who have very kindly permitted me to visit their lovely house on several occasions to look through the Campden Trust's superb collection of old photographs and drawings. I would also like to thank Geoffrey Powell for his advice and suggestions; his extensive research into the history of Campden has been an invaluable source of information. I am indebted to Alan Crawford and Fiona MacCarthy for their detailed knowledge of the work of Ashbee and the Guild of Handicraft in Chipping Campden. Jaqueline Mitchell of Alan Sutton Publishing, Alan Bell of The London Library, and the staff of Chipping Campden Library, Birmingham Central Reference Library, Gloucestershire County Record Office and Cheltenham Art Gallery and Museums have also proved extremely helpful. I would like to thank The Society of Authors, as the literary representatives of the Estate of John Masefield, for permission to quote from two of Masefield's poems, and the Board of Trustees of the Victoria and Albert Museum for the quotes from Alec Miller's unpublished manuscript. I am most grateful to John Limbrey for the use of his excellent map of Campden, the Campden Trust and the Campden and District Historical and Archaeological Society, who have both kindly loaned photographs and other material, and the Hunterian Art Gallery, University of Glasgow for permission to reproduce the photograph from the Mackintosh Collection. I am particularly grateful to Felicity Ashbee for her permission to quote from Ashbee's *Journal* and also reproduce the photograph of C.R. Ashbee by Frank Lloyd Wright. Finally, I would like give a special thanks to Frank Johnson for his advice, local knowledge and generosity.

Catherine Gordon
July 1993

Introduction

At the market place I stood in silent astonishment.
From end to end nobody was seen. My foot alone on the
gilded pavement [all consisting then not of cement
but of the dove-grey lias stone] had broken the
quiet of immemorial sleep and my own sounds only had
echoed around me. Between the church tower and the sun
lay the antique town in one graceful curve of what
seemed infinite detail and variety yet of matchless
harmony. Built all of stone, turned absolutely to gold
just then, this wide street widened still more midway
to admit, as islands, the arched pillared and gabled
Market Hall and the Gothically buttressed Guildhall.
It was indescribable, simply a dream.

Algernon Gissing, *The Footway Path in Gloucestershire*,
London, 1924.

This was how Algernon Gissing recalled his first visit to Chipping Campden back in 1890. First impressions are notoriously unreliable, but what Gissing described with such eloquence and emotion was, and still remains, a reasonably accurate picture of this historic Cotswold town. Only the silence of the deserted market place strikes an unfamiliar note today, but in Gissing's time this was probably due as much to the contemporary agricultural depression as the romantic image of rural tranquillity he wished to convey. For since Campden's heyday during the prosperous years of the medieval wool trade, the town's fortunes had fluctuated and diminished, and by the 1890s it supported a population of only around 1500 people and many of its buildings lay empty and derelict. However, its relative isolation from industrial society had ensured that its traditional way of life remained intact; its small community was still presided over by the clergy and landed gentry, and the lives of the townspeople remained regulated by the agricultural seasons, the local festivals and market days. Yet the town was unlikely to resist change for much longer. The railway had reached Campden in 1853 and brought an increasing range of goods into the shops, and the telegraph had been installed in 1886. More importantly, the first visitors had begun to arrive and it was only a matter of time before Chipping Campden was attracting a similarly fashionable clientele as the neighbouring village of Broadway. As it happened, the town's revival was to be guided by a more unexpected and beneficial source. In 1902 C.R. Ashbee, the Arts and Crafts designer and architect, moved his Guild of Handicraft from London's East End to Chipping Campden, and during the next six years was to transform its social and cultural life. It was a remarkably brave venture and, arguably, a great imposition, but it helped nurture a new sense of pride among the people of Campden in their historic town and its folk and craft traditions. Several influential and talented artists and craftsmen settled in Campden during this period, among them the etcher and draughtsman, F.L. Griggs, and it was primarily due to his efforts that the town succeeded in resisting the worst effects of twentieth-century tourism so that Gissing's poetic vision can still be appreciated today.

The photographs are credited as follows:

CT   Photographs in the possession of the Campden Trust.
CADHAS   Photographs and other material in the possession of the Campden and District Historical and Archaeological Society.
BCLH   Drawings reproduced from C.R. Ashbee's *A Book of Cottages and Little Houses*.

Decorated wagon from the Whitsuntide procession through the High Street, *c.* 1925.   CT

CHAPTER ONE

The Gift of the Golden Fleece

The town of Chipping Campden is situated in the county of Gloucestershire and nestles within a small fold of marlstone at the northern end of the Cotswold Hills.

Although pre-historic and Romano-British settlements abound throughout the region, no substantial evidence has yet been found of any settlement at Chipping Campden that dates before the Saxon period. However, the Whiteway, the ancient trackway that runs from Cirencester across the back of the wolds to Stratford-upon-Avon, passes through the town and may indicate that it dates from an earlier time.

The name Campden is undoubtedly of Saxon origin, as are most of the place-names in the surrounding area, and is a development of the word 'Campa-dene', a valley with fields or enclosures, the 'Campa' being derived from the plural of the Roman word 'campus' or field. The prefix 'Chipping' is a derivation of the Old English 'ceping', a market or market-place, and was added during the medieval period, probably during the early thirteenth century after the town had been granted its market charter, and it has been discarded and revived several times since.

Chipping Campden was certainly a well-established settlement by the seventh century, for the thirteenth-century chronicler Pierre de Langtoft was to record that a Council of Kings was held in Campden around AD 689 under the direction of King Ina of Wessex. By the time of the Norman Conquest its parish boundaries were probably clearly defined, as a charter granted by King Aethelred of c. 1005 confirms the award of land at Mickleton to the Benedictine Monastery at Eynsham, and describes the boundaries in detail including those 'of the people of Campden'. Chipping Campden's entry in the Domesday Book would also suggest that this was the case for it reads: 'The same Earl holds Campadene in Wideles hundred, Earl Harold held it. There are 15 hides taxed. In demesne are six plow tillages. There are 12 servi and 2 mills of 6s 2d, and two ancillae. It was worth £30 – now only £20.' The 'same Earl' is generally assumed to have been Hugh d'Avranches, Earl of Chester and nephew of King William. Although many fine Norman churches survive in the Cotswolds, at Blockley, Avening and Elkstone for example, little evidence remains of the Norman church that stood in Campden, as a

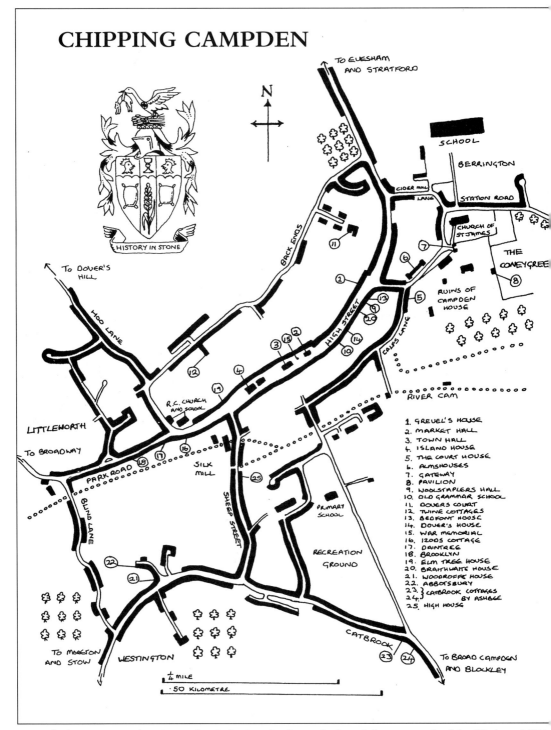

Map of Chipping Campden. Drawn by Catherine Gordon and adapted from a map by John Limbrey MSIA published in Jubilee Year 1977.

South doorway of the Norman Chapel, Broad Campden after its restoration and conversion in 1905–6.   CT

major rebuilding took place in the thirteenth century and obliterated all but a few fragments, among them an unusual corbel embellished with a muzzled bear that is now kept in the muniment room. However, in the adjacent hamlet of Broad Campden, the substantial remains of a small church can be found that date from the late eleventh or early twelfth centuries. This was dedicated to St Mary Magdalene and probably belonged to the Abbots of Tewkesbury, but during either the fourteenth or fifteenth centuries it was converted into a dwelling.

The rebuilding of Chipping Campden church during the thirteenth century would suggest that the town had begun to grow in size and importance by this time, and it is likely that this is when the High Street was laid out in its present form, probably by Hugh de Gondeville, who had been

3

Recent aerial photograph of Chipping Campden. Copyright of Cambridge University.   CADHAS

Sheep being driven through the High Street on their way to market, *c.* 1910.　CT

granted the manor of Campden in the late twelfth century. The long and gentle curve of the High Street is one of Campden's most important and appealing features, for it runs from its north-east end right through the centre of the town, and from there its curved outline is extended along Park Road to form the literal backbone of the settlement. It is possible that it may follow the route of a much earlier road, although it has also been suggested that the layout was ingeniously planned to protect the townspeople from the bitter winds that swept down off the surrounding hills. The street is broad in general, probably to accommodate the large flocks of sheep that were driven through the town, partly terraced with its western side set at a higher level, and also significantly wider towards its south-west end where the market-place is situated. This has the advantage of drawing the elongated settlement together, and the entire scheme provides an interesting example of early medieval town planning. Numerous burgage plots ran from the main street to Back Ends on the north-west side and to the River Cam on the south-east side, several of which now form long back gardens, and on these the traders, craftsmen and other townspeople built their timber huts. By 1247 the town had a weekly market, three annual fairs, and had even been visited by royalty. Henry II is recorded to have been in Campden in 1187 when he granted the town its first charter, and Henry III is also said to have been to the town on at least three occasions to confirm this charter. Apart from the two churches,

Thirteenth-century dovecote at Westington Old Manor.   CT

only one building in the parish appears to have survived from this period, and that is the small, stone dovecote at Westington Old Manor, a house believed to date back to 1273.

During the fourteenth century Chipping Campden entered upon a period of outstanding influence and prosperity that was to last for the following two hundred years. Sheep-farming had been common to the region since the Roman occupation, and most of the large villas so far discovered in the Cotswolds were associated with agriculture, and with sheep-rearing in particular. As early as 1080 the first wool-merchants' guild had been established at Burford, and the wool trade rapidly developed during the medieval period to become the primary source of England's wealth. This was due to a number of factors, such as the sharp decrease in population caused by famine, economic recession and disease (notably the Black Death of 1348),

Sheep-shearing with hand-driven flexible drive shears, *c.* 1910.   CT

which meant that much arable land reverted to pasture; and there was also an increased demand for wool from mainland Europe, especially Italy and the Low Countries. During the fourteenth century Edward III succeeded in creating a virtual monopoly in the trade, and even used the threat of preventing the export of wool to Flanders as a bargaining weapon at the start of the Hundred Years War. The Cotswolds became the most important centre of production quite simply as it produced the finest wool. Its sheep were descended from the Roman Longwools, bred to provide a heavy fleece of long-haired or stapled wool, and it also had the best sheep runs and a fine road system inherited from the Romans along which the laden pack-trains could transport the wool to the south coast ports. Chipping Campden quickly acquired a reputation as one of the chief wool-dealing towns in the region to which the wool was brought from all over the Midlands and the Welsh Marches to be sorted, packed, purchased and despatched. As an indication of the scale of the trade handled by the Campden staplers, it would appear that the local merchant, William Weoley, was owed the enormous sum of £1,180 by the Albertine Wool Company of Florence, and he had to enlist the help of Henry VI to recover the money. Restrictive practices and the requisition and sale of wool undoubtedly enabled merchants to make, and occasionally lose, vast amounts of money and many local men became very rich indeed. Much of this wealth was lavished on new buildings, in particular the fine parish churches in the region, which served to salve the conscience of many dishonest woolmen after a lifetime of dubious dealing, and also gave the

Fourteenth-century traceried panels on the buttresses of the nineteenth-century Town Hall.
CT

Cotswold masons ample opportunity to demonstrate their admirable skills. They were fortunate in that there were abundant supplies of local oolitic limestone with which to practise their craft. It is a remarkably accommodating building stone that ranges in colour from creamy-buff to brownish-amber and weathers to a warm, silvery grey, but above all has the special quality of being able to reflect changing intensities of light to produce a wonderful richness and variety of hue. Most Cotswold villages had their own quarry, and Chipping Campden was no exception as much of the town is built from stone from the quarry above Westington, dragged down the hill by a team of oxen to be shaped and dressed by the local masons. Three important buildings in the High Street date from this period. The first of these is the Town Hall, which retains panels of traceried fourteenth-century stonework in some of its buttresses, and may have been a wool exchange or a court house of the burgessess of the borough. Medieval stonework found in other buildings in the town was probably removed from the structure when it was rebuilt by Richard Hulls in the early nineteenth-century. At the opposite end of the High Street is the Woolstaplers Hall, a late fourteenth-century building that was built for Robert Calf, a wool merchant, whose family also gave their

Grevel's House, High Street, home of Campden's most famous wool merchant.   CT

name to the lane that runs parallel to the south-east side of the High Street. The building may have been a meeting-house for the woolstaplers or a wool exchange and had certainly become the Guildhall by the eighteenth century. Inside is a splendid medieval oak roof and a fireplace carved with the rebus of the Calf family. Opposite Woolstaplers Hall is Grevel's House, the home of Campden's most successful woolstapler, William Grevel, who reached such heights of influence that he was to become financier to Richard II. Grevel was the son of a local man, Richard Grevel, and in 1367 he bought a house and land in Campden for ten marks. By 1380 he had accumulated such wealth that he decided to build himself another house on a prominent site at the northern end of the town. The house is a particularly fine example of its type and was originally arranged around a large courtyard, but probably its best-known feature is the impressive two-storey Perpendicular bay window with its cinquefoil-headed lights, traceried panelling and gargoyles that looks towards the church. By 1397 Grevel had also bought the manor of Milcote, near Stratford-upon-Avon, from Sir Walter Beauchamp and, after his death in 1401, Grevel's descendants continued to prosper and they acquired Warwick Castle in 1605 and were later made Earls of Warwick. Although William Grevel is traditionally credited with being the chief benefactor of the rebuilding of the parish church, in fact much of the work was carried out in the early fourteenth century when he was still a youth and the later

Campden parish church during the snow of January 1947.   CADHAS

Perpendicular additions were executed at least fifty to a hundred years after his death. Admittedly he left one hundred marks to the church when he died, but this was only to be expected and it is known that at least one other local merchant, William Bradway (d. 1488), left a similar sum towards the rebuilding of the nave. The brasses in the church commemorate several other such benefactors including William Weoley (or Welley d. 1540), John Lethanard (d. 1467), and William Gybbs (d. 1484). However Grevel's brass is by far the most impressive and it makes the somewhat immodest claim that he was 'the flower of the wool merchants of all England'.

Chipping Campden church stands on slightly raised ground to the northeast of the High Street. It was originally dedicated to Our Lady or Blessed Virgin but during the mid-fifteenth century, after the Dissolution of the Monasteries and other associated measures carried out by Henry VIII, it was re-dedicated to St James the Great. The rebuilding of the mid-thirteenth century included the extension of the Norman chancel, now marked by a tomb recess on the north side, but the main evidence of thirteenth-century work is to be found in the south doorway and much of the south wall, although this has since been refaced. The crypt was most probably an ossuary and has two naves, each of three bays, with quadripartite vaulting on octagonal shafts. Early in the fourteenth century another extensive rebuilding programme began, which included the addition of the south aisle and the north chapel – although the north wall of the chapel does include stonework from an earlier period. Some time later the south aisle was buttressed, the chancel was rebuilt and extended, and the north aisle and the south porch were added. During the latter half of the fifteenth century, as Chipping Campden reached the peak of its prosperity and influence, the second stage of the work began which developed the piecemeal medieval structure into the fine Perpendicular building that survives today. The south chapel was built on, the windows of the south aisle were opened up, and a new nave was skilfully inserted between the aisles with clerestory windows that are carried across the chancel arch. It is very similar to the nave at Northleach church, built around thirty years earlier, and is very probably by the same master mason. The exterior of the building was cleverly amalgamated by the addition of embattled parapets with crocketed pinnacles that give a decorative flourish to all the walls, and the windows were heightened and provided with dripmoulds with stops. One pair of stops is carved with heads and David Verey has suggested that the mitred head dress of the lady indicates a date of between 1445 and 1465. Finally, the superb tower was built on, which soars to a height of over 37 metres. It is divided into three main stages, the upper stages of which have openings with ogee heads and finials, and each face is also divided vertically by thin pilaster strips which form two ogee arches across the embattled parapet and are surmounted by small pinnacles. At each corner of the tower are set diagonal buttresses and these terminate in tall, crocketed pinnacles which give the tower its distinctive profile. Medieval fittings within the church include a fifteenth-century piscina and credence shelf, a triple sedilia with cusped arches, vaulted canopies and late Gothic cresting, and also half of a bowl of a Norman font, which is fixed to the east wall of the south aisle. The present font is an 1839 copy of the fifteenth-century font in St Mary Magdalene, Oxford, but the lectern is an original fifteenth-century piece. This was given to the church by Sir Baptist Hicks in the early seventeenth century together with the early sixteenth-century pulpit. Regrettably, the chancel screen is missing and only fragments of medieval glass survive, both of which were probably victims of Puritan iconoclasm. Of particular interest are the medieval vestments displayed in the tower, notably the fifteenth-century crimson velvet cope embroidered with powdered coronets and saints beneath canopies, and also the late fifteenth-century altar hangings embroidered with the Virgin and Angels. These are believed to be the one complete set to survive in England and they were copied for the hangings in Westminster Abbey for the Coronation of Elizabeth II. Among the several memorials to important Campden figures is a large monument to Thomas Smyth (d. 1593). This has a recumbent effigy in armour lying upon a tomb chest carved with effigies of his two wives and

Interior of Campden church.   CT

Embroidered altar hangings of *c.* 1450 in Campden church. Copied for the hangings of Westminster Abbey on the occasion of the Coronation of Elizabeth II.   CADHAS

thirteen children, and a Renaissance canopy above carved with ornate strapwork. On a much grander scale is the monument to Sir Baptist Hicks, Lord Campden (d. 1629) and his wife in the Earl of Gainsborough's family chapel. The recumbent effigies of Hicks and his wife recline in their state robes upon a black marble tomb chest beneath a canopy supported by twelve columns of Egyptian marble. The detail of this monument is of such outstanding quality that it may well be the work of Nicholas Stone.

Chipping Campden church is rightly regarded as one of the finest Perpendicular buildings in the region – but it was only just completed in time. By the fifteenth century the nature of the wool trade slowly began to change, and the export of raw wool began to decline in favour of the export of manufactured cloth. Between the thirteenth and fourteenth centuries exported wool had amounted to some 30,000 sacks a year, but between 1348 and 1400 the number had fallen to around 19,000, while the number of bales of finished cloths exported had risen from just under 4,500 to almost 45,000. This decline was largely due to the general fall in the price of agricultural goods, changing fashion and the import of dyed Spanish wool and other new materials. Eventually an Act of Parliament restricted wool-dealing to specific towns in the Inland Staple from which Campden was excluded and, despite a petition of 1617 by the bailiffs and burgesses of the town, it was not long before the upland wool trade had ceased altogether to be replaced by the clothing industry based in the valleys around Stroud and Painswick.

13

CHAPTER TWO

The New Rule

During the early years of the fifteenth century, when the town's prosperity was at its peak, Chipping Campden was not owned by a single landowner but divided into two, one part being held by Thomas de Stafford, who had inherited it from his uncle, Edward de Stafford, Bishop of Exeter, and the other part held by Edward de Ludlow. Throughout the following century the manor of Campden changed hands several times, but it remained divided and it was not until the sixteenth century that it was united once more. In 1536 Thomas Smyth married Elizabeth Fitzherbert, a descendant of Edward de Ludlow, and thereby acquired half of the manor. He was a very wealthy and influential figure, who became a member of the King's Council for the Marches of Wales, a JP for Gloucestershire and was also twice appointed Sheriff of Gloucestershire in 1571 and 1583. By a series of shrewd purchases Smyth managed to acquire the entire Domesday manor, with the exception of a few freehold plots and the hamlet of Broad Campden; these were later purchased by his son, Anthony, who succeeded him in 1593. The Smyth family moved into the manor house at Berrington and attempted to establish their authority on the town. However, according to Geoffrey Powell, they met with little success, and Smyth became so unpopular that the townspeople raided his property and even sent armed retainers to prevent his men grazing cattle on common pastureland.

In 1547, during Smyth's residency in Campden, the town was described by the Charity Commissioners as a parish of 600 houseling people, with a church, two manor courts, a market, several fair days, justice courts and also a Grammar School. The school had been founded in 1440 with an endowment provided by John Fereby and his wife Margery. Fereby was a Surrey magnate, who had fought at Agincourt and had been appointed head of the Custom of Wool Hides and Wool-fells in 1410. He was born in the Campden area and also knew the town through his work for the Custom, which would probably explain why he chose to establish a free school there. It is not known for certain where the original school stood but it is possible that the former Grammar School building in the High Street was built on the site of the original schoolhouse.

Early seventeenth-century schoolroom of the Grammar School with classical niche containing a bust of either John Fereby or Sir Baptist Hicks.   CT

The Dissolution of the Monasteries had released vast acreages of land between 1536 and 1539 and this stimulated a great surge of secular building in the region which led to the flowering of the Cotswold building tradition. During this period Chipping Campden was to acquire many new attractive stone and timber-framed buildings, for example the Old Kings Arms, Peyton House (refronted in stone in the eighteenth century) and Combe House (now Campden House) on the outskirts of the town. However, the corruption and misrule of the Tudor monarchy also created a rapid inflation of property prices and many landlords were either ruined or made fortunes. Religious and educational establishments were particularly vulnerable to the

The Almshouses, built by Sir Baptist Hicks in 1612.   CT

mis-management or greed of ruthless local entrepreneurs. In 1563 a consistory court in Chipping Campden complained about the lack of a good bible in the parish, the ruinous state of the churchyard, and the disrespectful attitude of the Campden parishioners, in particular 'somme there be that do not receive the communion as often as permissable' and that 'taulke and jangle at service tyme'. Further problems occurred around 1573 when the trustees of the Grammar School began to plunder its endowments and thus deprive the school of vital funds. Smyth's unpopularity can have done little to alleviate the situation, and it was no doubt with some relief and apprehension that the Campden people welcomed the arrival of Sir Baptist Hicks.

Like Smyth, Hicks was a self-made man of considerable wealth, who came from a Gloucestershire family of money-lenders and dealers in luxury textiles. His brother Michael had become influential in the court of Elizabeth I, and Baptist Hicks was to provide her successor, James I, and most of his court, with financial support, reputedly of sums as large as £150,000. It was this that made him his vast fortune and he was knighted on James I's accession in 1603. Between 1606 and 1609 Hicks bought the manor of Campden from Anthony

The Market Hall, Chipping Campden built by Sir Baptist Hicks in 1627.   CT

Smyth and, in 1610, also bought the nearby estate of Weston Park, no doubt to fully establish himself among the local gentry. In 1612 he built himself a substantial house in London, Campden House in Kensington, but Chipping Campden was where he chose to spend much of his time, and he lavished vast sums of money on the town and became closely involved with the lives of the townspeople. Due to his generosity the church was repaired, the chancel roof was leaded, and a gallery, pulpit and lectern installed inside, while outside the churchyard was tidied up and a wall built around its perimeter. In 1612 he built the block of almshouses a short distance from the church, probably on the site of an earlier foundation, at a cost of £1,000 to provide homes for six men and six women of the parish. The building was designed in the shape of an 'I' as a compliment to his monarch, with the central range divided into eight gabled bays and detailed with tall, paired chimneys, ovolo-mullioned windows and Tudor-arched doorways in a simple but dignified rendering of the Cotswold style. Water was piped down to the almshouses from the small, ogee-roofed conduit house on Westington Hill, which later supplied Hicks's own house as well. In his will he left land at Charingworth worth £140 a year for the upkeep of the almshouses, in addition to a weekly pension of 3s 4d and fuel and clothing for the inmates. Other acts of benevolence included rescuing the School from further deterioration when, in 1626, he removed the unscrupulous trustees and managed to recover some of the

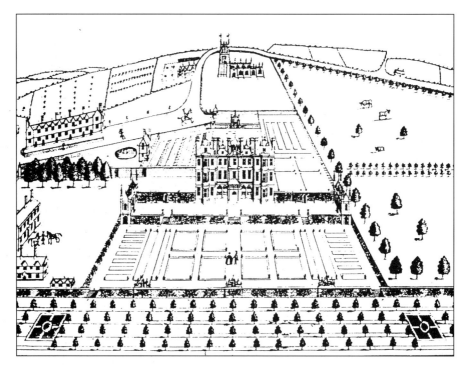

Campden House from an eighteenth-century drawing in the British Museum.   CADHAS

misappropriated money. With all or part of this recovered money, he built a new school in the High Street, only the schoolroom of which survived the remodelling of 1863 by C.A. Buckler, and above the fireplace is a classical niche containing a bust of either Fereby or Hicks. In 1627 Sir Baptist Hicks built the Market Hall in the centre of the High Street at a cost of £90, which for many years housed the butter, cheese and egg market, and with its sturdy arcades, small gables and squat profile it has become one of the most popular features of the town centre. Campden House, the magnificent Jacobean mansion that Sir Baptist built for himself adjacent to the church, would have been his chief architectural contribution not merely to Chipping Campden but to the nation as a whole. Work began on the house in 1613 and, including its furnishings, it is believed to have cost as much as £44,000, which gives some idea of Sir Baptist's extraordinary wealth. Unfortunately, the building was destroyed by fire during the Civil War just three decades after it was built and no attempt was made to repair the damage. An eighteenth-century drawing of the house in the British Museum shows it to have been a substantial building in the Cotswold Jacobean style, with an

Gateway to Campden House, blocked till earlier this century to prevent the theft of stone from the site.   CT

ornate roofline and domed cupola, surrounded by elaborate gardens and garden buildings. Two garden pavilions or banqueting houses escaped the fire, together with the garden terraces and some outbuildings, among them the lodges and gateway adjacent to the church. These two, small, square buildings are surmounted by ogee-domed ashlar roofs and finials, and are linked by a curtain wall with a shaped parapet that conceals chimneys in its finials. The central arched carriageway is set beneath a pediment with Sir Baptist's coat of arms in the tympanum and would have formed a splendid and fitting entrance to the mansion. It seems very likely that if the house had survived it would have been one of the showpieces of the region, although it may well have had a detrimental effect on the scale and character of the town.

In 1628 Sir Baptist was created Baron Hicks of Ilmington and Viscount Campden of Campden but died the following year at Old Jewry. As he had no male heir, he had already secured the reversion of his titles to Edward Noel, Baron Noel of Kidlington, the husband of his eldest daughter Juliana, whose grandson was to become the first Earl of Gainsborough. The manor

Dover's Hill. Site of the famous Cotswold Games.   CT

has descended continuously through the Noel family to the present day and, although they have estates elsewhere, some members of the family still live in the town.

It was during Sir Baptist's lifetime that the famous Dover's Games were first held on the area of common land known as Kingcombe Plain, west of Chipping Campden, part of which is now called Dover's Hill. Robert Dover was a lawyer and estate agent, who moved to Saintbury in the early seventeenth century and, around 1611, he decided to re-organize a series of existing minor festivities known as the Whitsun Ales into a major annual gathering to be held on the Thursday and Friday of Whitsun week. The events included horse-racing, hare-coursing and wrestling accompanied by games of chess and cards, music, dancing and feasting, which all took place around a realistic model of Dover Castle and were presided over by Dover, seated upon a white horse. The Games quickly established a reputation throughout the region and even inspired a book of indifferent poetry, the *Annalia Dubrensia* published in 1636, in which they were described somewhat optimistically as 'Olimpick' – in truth they were usually an excuse for much drunkenness, gambling and rioting, and the athletic prowess of the contestants was a relatively minor consideration. Nevertheless, such was their reputation that even Shakespeare is believed to have referred to them in his much-quoted words from the first scene of *The Merry Wives of Windsor*: 'How does your fallow greyhound, sir? I heard say he was outrun on Cotsall.' At the

ANNALIA
DVBRENSIA.

Vpon the yeerely celebration of
Mr. ROBERT DOVERS Climpick
Games vpon *Cotſwold-Hills.*

Written by

MICHAELL DRAYTON.	Eſq.	IOHN TRVSSELL.	Gent.
IOHN TRVSSELL.	Gent.	WILLIAM COLE.	Gent.
V. ILLIAM DVRHAM. Oxon,		FERRIMAN RVTTER. Oxon.	
WILLIAM DENNY	Eſq.	IOHN STRATFORD.	Gent.
THOMAS RANDALL. Cant.		THOMAS SANFORD.	Gent.
BEN : IOHNSON.		ROBERT GRIFFIN.	Gent.
IOHN DOVER.	Gent,	IOHN COLE.	Gent.
OWEN FELTHAM.	Gent.	ROBERT DVRHAM. Oxon.	
FRANCIS IZOD.	Gent,	A SIRINX Oxon.	
NICHOLAS WALLINGTON. Ox.		IOHN MONSON.	Eſq.
IOHN BALLARD. Oxon.		WALTON POOLE.	Gent.
TIMOTHY OGLE.	Gent.	RICHARD WELLS. Oxon.	
WILLIAM AMBROSE. Oxon.		WILLIAM FORTH.	Eſq.
WILLIAM BELLAS.	Gent.	SHACK : MARMYON.	Gent.
THOMAS COLE. Oxon.		R N.	
WILLIAM BASSE.	Gent.	THOMAS HEYWOOD.	Gent.
CAPTAINE MENESE.			

LONDON,
Printed by *Robert Raworth,* for *Mathew Walbancke.* 1636.

Title page of the *Annalia Dubrensis.*
CADHAS

outbreak of the Civil War the Games had to be abandoned, but they were revived after the Restoration and continued to be held for the next two hundred years, by which time they were attracting vast crowds of some 30,000 people, mainly from the industrial cities. However, there was increasing opposition to the drunkenness and violence that occurred, particularly the introduction of such sports as shin-kicking and backsword fighting, and in 1852 it was arranged that all the remaining open fields and common land on Dover's Hill that fell within the parish of Weston-sub-Edge should be enclosed to bring an end to the Games. Despite these efforts the Games still continued on a much smaller scale as part of a Wake held annually in the town, and were eventually revived in their original form as part of the celebrations of the Festival of Britain in 1951.

The Civil War did not take long to reach Chipping Campden. The Hicks family were fervent Royalists and, after Charles I besieged Gloucester in 1643, the town soon became vulnerable as it was situated on the direct route from Gloucester to Warwick, both of which were Parliamentary strongholds. It was garrisoned by the summer of 1643 and again in December of the following year, when Campden House was also fortified under the command of Sir Henry Bard. In May 1645 Bard and his men were summoned by the King to join him on his march to Naseby, but before they left they burnt the house,

COTSWOLD GAMES.

Frontispiece of the *Annalia Dubrensis*.   CADHAS

Elm Tree House, High Street.   CT

most probably to deny it to the enemy, and Lady Juliana was forced to move into a converted stable block (now The Court House). After this seemingly wanton gesture there was to be no respite. On 24 June, Sir Thomas Fairfax marched 11,500 Parliamentarian troops through the town causing untold damage, and soon after, on 7 September, the King also passed through the town on his way to raise the siege of Hereford. The following March the Campden people had to contend with a large Roundhead force based in the town and endure the consequences of innumerable minor skirmishes that occurred on the surrounding hillsides. The Restoration was understandably a time of great rejoicing and the churchwardens' accounts record that a generous sum of 3s was paid to the Campden bellringers to ring out the good news over the parish. However the celebrations were to be overshadowed by the occurrence of a mysterious tragedy known as 'The Campden Wonder', which has since become the source of endless speculation among many eminent writers, lawyers and historians. One night in August 1660, John Harrison, Lady Juliana's elderly steward, disappeared while collecting rents at Ebrington. A blood-stained hat band and comb were discovered and Harrison's servant John Perry was soon arrested for murder. He protested his

The Martins, High Street.   CT

innocence and proceeded to accuse both his mother and brother of the crime, and eventually all three of them were hanged on Broadway Hill. Two years later Harrison reappeared and claimed that he had been kidnapped, sold to Turkish pirates and then miraculously escaped. This seems a highly improbable story, and it is more likely that Harrison was involved in some Restoration plot and the death of Perry may have been necessary to silence him. Harrison's wife committed suicide two years after her husband's return and this would also suggest that the plot was more complicated than it appeared.

Clifton House, High Street.   CT

Apart from this unfortunate incident the Restoration brought a time of peace and stability to the town. Throughout the region the new squirearchy provided a fresh source of employment on the improvement of their estates, and it was during this period that the quarrying industry reached its peak in response to the demand for quality stone for the rebuilding of London and Warwick, after the Fires of 1666 and 1694 respectively, and for the construction of large houses, such as Badminton House, Blenheim Palace and Cirencester Park. Among the most highly-regarded mason-builders of the day were the Woodward family of Chipping Campden, who were also involved with the construction of many of the fine houses built in the High Street for the wealthier yeomen and tradesmen during this period. Most of these houses are of an exceptional quality and contribute much to the character of the town. Among the earliest of them were Elm Tree House of

Bedfont House, High Street.   CT

1656 and Green Dragons (formerly Robert's House) dated 1691; by the
early eighteenth century classical influences became more pronounced on
buildings such as The Martins and Clifton House, and many older timber-
framed buildings such as Charlcote and Peyton House were upgraded with
eighteenth-century façades. Particularly striking are Dover's House, a simply-
detailed and well-proportioned design of two storeys and five bays with
Venetian windows to its garden elevation, and Bedfont House, a building of
exceptional quality and sophisticated detail by Thomas Woodward for the
Cotterell family that dates from the 1740s and has fluted Corinthian pilasters,
a balustraded parapet and an elegant doorcase embellishing its street
elevation. The town also grew considerably in size during the Georgian
period for, according to the contemporary local historian, Sir Robert
Atkyns, it had 347 houses and 1,464 inhabitants by this time. These figures
were to change little over the next hundred years or so as, despite the general
rise in population, many Campden people began to migrate to the industrial
towns in search of work.

The Cotswold countryside around Chipping Campden also began to alter
significantly during the eighteenth century as the Enclosure Acts caused vast

acreages of land to be divided up by stone walls and fencing. Large new farmsteads were built to service the new allocations of land created from the former scattered holdings that could be managed far more efficiently and take advantage of improved methods of agriculture to further increase their profits. Deprived of their common grazing rights, some smallholders became landless labourers, and many left the area or turned to cottage industry for a living. The Enclosure Act for Chipping Campden was not passed till 1799 but as a result over one quarter of the parish, some 3,281 acres, were divided up, and six new farmhouses were built. The increase in rural poverty appears to have affected the town quite severely as, according to Geoffrey Powell, the cost of poor relief rose from £200 at the end of the seventeenth century to over £1,000 a hundred years later, and to over £2,000 by the early nineteenth century. Apart from farming and quarrying, a few small industries provided an additional source of employment. Many of the local women made knitted stockings, baskets, kid-gloves and stays in their own homes for sale elsewhere, and there was a rope and sack-making workshop in Back Ends (now known as Twine Cottages), which also provided work in the fields growing the flax and hemp, as well as in the flax mill, which employed as many as 40 people in 1838. Chipping Campden also benefited from the silk trade which flourished in the North Cotswolds during the eighteenth century, particularly in the nearby village of Blockley, where several twisting and throwing mills were established mainly to service the Coventry ribbon trade. In 1710 a silk-throwing mill was built in Sheep Street, but this had ceased production by around 1859 when the trade was destroyed by the import of high quality silks from India and France. There were also a few enterprising individuals who sought an alternative approach to impending poverty and destitution. One such entrepreneur was Jonathan Hulls, a farmer from Broad Campden, who recognized the potential of the low-pressure steam engine, previously used only for mine-pumping, and in 1737 he filed a patent for the engine and built the first steamship on the River Avon at Evesham. The boat sank, but Hulls' inventive spirit was undaunted by this failure and, with his two friends Richard Darby, a local maltster, and William Bradford, the writing master at the Grammar School, he went on to produce a guide for gauging salt, a slide-rule and a rather curious instrument intended for the identification of counterfeit gold and the prevention of its fraudulent use.

During the first half of the nineteenth century Chipping Campden still appeared little affected by the pace and progress of the industrial age. The 1801 census records a total of 1,479 inhabitants, little change in population since Sir Robert Atkyns' visit, but as the century progressed the Campden people were obliged to make some adjustments to their traditional way of life. The two manor courts were abandoned as their duties had become severely

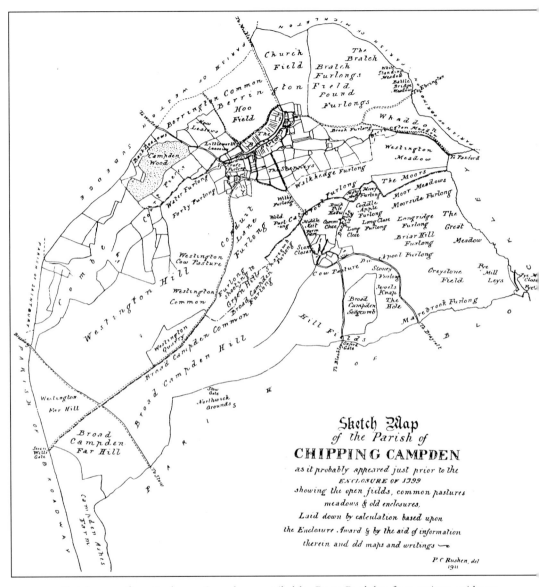

Sketch map of pre-Enclosure Campden compiled by Percy Rushden from written evidence, c. 1911.

restricted by the Enclosure Act, and by the 1840s it was considered necessary to install six policemen in a station at the corner of Leysbourne and Cider Mill Lane to combat the rise in crime. However the ancient Corporation was maintained until 1883 when it was abolished by the Municipal Corporations Act, but it was not replaced by the parish council till 1894. The town's

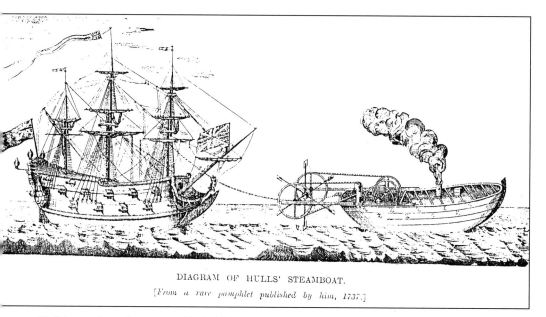

DIAGRAM OF HULLS' STEAMBOAT.
[*From a rare pamphlet published by him, 1737.*]

Hulls' steam boat, from a pamphlet published by him in 1737.   CADHAS

education arrangements were also improved. In 1710 money had been given to the town by Lord Weymouth on behalf of his brother James Thynne of Buckland, 'to instruct and clothe 30 poor girls of the parish'. It is uncertain where the girls were educated at first, but by 1820 they attended the Blue Coat School set up in the present County Library building, although by 1831 the school had moved to Grevel House and the Library building had become an infants' school. A school for boys was built in Church Street in 1837 and is now used as church rooms.

Improvements in communications also began to have their effect. By 1800 there was a regular carrier service to London, and over the next few decades local turnpike trusts were set up to maintain the local roads and three toll houses were built on the outskirts of the town. Canal transport brought few benefits as the nearest canals passed through Stratford and Evesham and heavy goods then had to be brought to the town by road. This was to have some advantages though as the town continued to use the local building materials rather than Welsh slates and cheap brick brought in from elsewhere and as a result its architectural character remained intact. However, when the railway finally arrived in 1853, it seemed probable that life in Campden would change for good.

CHAPTER THREE

C.R. Ashbee and the Guild of Handicraft

Work began on the Oxford, Worcester and Wolverhampton Railway line in 1845. Brunel was in charge of the operation, much to his deep regret as the project became renowned for the countless delays caused by obstructive landowners. In Chipping Campden itself he was forced to alter his original scheme to bring the line right into the town near the Volunteer Inn in Park Road, due as much to the steep gradients as resistance from the townspeople, and it was finally agreed to build the station a mile and a half out of town on the Paxford Road. This arrangement fortunately gave Chipping Campden all the convenience of an excellent railway service without loss to its essentially peaceful rural character and, as a result, the area began to attract welcome new investment. For example, not far from Chipping Campden, the Redesdales built Batsford Park between 1888 and

The Volunteer Inn, Park Road.   CT

Campden Station, built in 1853 and demolished in 1966.   CADHAS

1893, and on the outskirts of the town, Combe House was rebuilt for the Noel family in 1846 by the architect R.C. Carpenter in an ornate Victorian Gothic style (including a window designed by Pugin of *c.* 1850 which has since been removed), with gardens and terraces laid out by Sir Thomas Nasmith. It was to become the new Campden House, and once installed the Noel family became closely involved with life in the town once more.

Such projects helped to provide some local employment and on the larger estates there were additional benefits such as new schools, estate housing, hospitals and village halls, but effects were very localized and did little to relieve the poverty that afflicted the region. Chipping Campden appeared to be surviving the depression with admirable fortitude. Queen Victoria's Jubilee was celebrated in grand style with a procession, sports, races, a great public dinner and a bonfire party up on Dover's Hill. In 1863 the Grammar School was rebuilt, a new police station was built in 1871, a Baptist church was built in 1872, and between 1875 and 1876 the parish church was restored by Waller & Wood of Gloucester. The vicar, Canon Kennaway, also built an attractive row of houses in Leysbourne for his outdoor staff. The prominent Roman Catholic community in the town opened a convent school in 1869, and in 1891 built a church nearby designed by William Lunn of Malvern. Although these new buildings helped to boost the town's morale, they could not mask the underlying insecurities imposed by the depression and with

31

The Grammar School as it was remodelled in 1863 by C.A. Buckler.   CT

hindsight they seemed only to emphasize the townspeople's commitment to the institutions which bound their traditional way of life together. It was certainly significant that Canon Kennaway's new cottages in Leysbourne were the only new domestic buildings to appear in the town centre during the second half of the century. Mechanization, falling prices and imports from abroad had all taken their toll and by the 1890s rural employers could no longer afford to pay their labourers a living wage. In 1904 C.R. Ashbee recorded that the population of Campden had dropped by 25 per cent in 30 years, and was to add that 'Other Cotswold villages would tell the same story and the little roofless houses and empty cottages to be seen . . . are the practical illustration of the economic fact.' However, the sad state of the rural economy was to prove to Chipping Campden's advantage in the long term as most of its buildings had escaped the worst excesses of Victorian restoration, despite the replacement of its old limestone paving by concrete in 1893.

When Ashbee first came to Chipping Campden in 1901 the town seemed to represent the ideal city of his romantic imagination, a 'City of the Sun', with its golden limestone buildings, medieval history, and strong sense of tradition. It may not have been quite so detached from the industrial world as he would have liked to believe, but he resolved to move his Guild there as

The new police station of 1871.   CT

soon as possible, and once Ashbee had made up his mind there was no turning back. Charles Robert Ashbee (1863–1942) was one of the leading figures of the Arts and Crafts Movement, which had emerged in response to the apparent deterioration of social and aesthetic standards in the aftermath of industrialization. These concerns were not new, for they had been expressed by several writers, designers and social theorists earlier in the century, such as Carlyle, Ruskin and Pugin, all of whom had opposed the appalling living and working conditions and the denial of personal creativity and individuality imposed by the factory system. Efforts to improve these standards by politicians and manufacturers were accompanied by a strong desire to emulate the medieval period in terms of creativity, craftsmanship and high quality design. William Morris was to develop these ideas and give fresh emphasis to the close association between social and aesthetic values, as he wrote: 'Men

The High Street in Ashbee's day.   CT

Wixey's grocery shop at the south end of the High Street.   CT

Photograph of C.R. Ashbee taken in
1900 by Frank Lloyd Wright.

living amongst such ugliness cannot conceive of beauty, and therefore cannot express it.' He firmly believed in the rights of the individual and the redemptive power of beauty, and he strove to cultivate aesthetic awareness and a sense of social responsibility in his writings, lectures and through the work of his firm, Morris & Co. Morris's ideas and the products of his firm had particular appeal to the affluent middle classes, who were eager to flaunt their social conscience and discerning taste, and as the demand for quality handmade goods increased, innumerable craft workshops and guilds became established throughout the country by both amateur and professional craftsmen. It was against this background that the Arts and Crafts Movement became established, an informal association of architects, artists, designers and craftsmen, who shared a strong social and moral conscience, and who sought to express their beliefs through their work, drawing inspiration from traditional rural crafts, vernacular building and the beauty of the English countryside.

Ashbee had emerged from a comfortable, if unusual middle-class background. He was a 'tall, slim, but muscular-looking man' with intense dark eyes, a large moustache and a disarming smile, a truly dynamic character driven by his social convictions and romantic idealism. He had attended Wellington School and then went to King's College, Cambridge, where he developed an interest in art and architecture and first read Ruskin. In 1886 he entered the architectual office of G.F. Bodley and, on the advice of his great friend the writer, lecturer and Socialist, Edward Carpenter, he went to live at Toynbee Hall, the pioneer university settlement in the East End of London. There he introduced a Ruskin reading class, which proved such a success that in 1888 he decided to found the Guild and School of Handicraft. At first the Guild had only three working craftsmen, and was organized on a co-operative basis with a profit-sharing system – more to give the Guildsmen a sense of involvement as the financial rewards were always somewhat theoretical. The School had 80 students in its first year, who were taught by Guild members, the idea being to allow the students to join the Guild once they had reached the required standard. Initially Ashbee took out a lease on a warehouse in 34 Commercial Street, but by 1890 he sought out larger premises at Essex House, a large eighteenth-century building in the Mile End Road. The School was forced to close down in 1895 due to financial problems, but the Guild flourished and was soon producing ten different crafts all with a distinctive style and identity, including printing on equipment acquired from Morris's Kelmscott Press. In 1898 the Guild was made into a limited liability company to place it on a more secure financial base and it also opened a shop at 16a Brook Street to help market its products. Four years later Ashbee was sufficiently confident to open a gallery nearby at 67a Bond Street, and regular exhibitions and articles in journals such as *The Studio* and *Dekorative Kunst* all helped to promote the Guild's work at home and abroad. By 1901 Ashbee was thinking about moving out of London to seek a more pleasant and humane working environment for his craftsmen, as he believed the squalor of the East End was draining their creative energies and in rural surroundings they would be able to spend their time away from the workbench in a more productive and fulfilling way. There were also practical considerations for the move. The Essex House lease was due to expire, it was necessary to expand the workshops, and Ashbee believed cheaper accommodation would be available in the countryside. He looked at sites in Kent, Letchworth and Blockley, and eventually went to look around Chipping Campden at the suggestion of his friend and business adviser, Rob Martin Holland, whose family home was at Overbury on the southern slopes of Bredon Hill. Chipping Campden seemed the ideal choice as, quite apart from the beauty of the place, there were numerous disused buildings to accommodate the Guild and a good railway service to London. The practical argument against uprooting all the Guildsmen and their families, some 150 people in all, from the centre of London to a remote Cotswold town did not seem to occur to him. After additional visits and a democratic vote, the Guild agreed to make the move, although a few craftsmen did choose to stay behind.

The old silk mill, Sheep Street, showing several of the Guildsmen looking out through the windows.   CT

By the spring of 1902 Ashbee had carried out a thorough survey of empty and derelict properties in Chipping Campden and made arrangements with Louis Dease, the Earl of Gainsborough's land agent, for their immediate occupation. The Guild was installed at the old silk mill in Sheep Street, which was leased at £40 a year and renamed Essex House, with showrooms and offices and the Essex House Press on the ground floor, jewellery, silversmithing and enamelling on the first floor, and cabinet-making, wood-working and french polishing on the second floor. The smithy was set up in an outhouse in the garden, and an oil-engine was installed in a garden shed as the mill-stream could not provide adequate power for the woodworking machinery. Ashbee established an architectural office at Elm Tree House and, between 1902 and 1904, the Essex House Press bindery was moved to Island House, which was also used as a social club after 1903. The Guild Library was temporarily stored in a room at Braithwaite House and plans were made to house the Guild Museum in the Grammar School. A cottage in the mill garden and a row of six cottages nearby were leased to the Guild to sub-let to the Guildsmen on a temporary basis, and other houses were either rented by

Woolstaplers Hall (with oriel window) and Braithwaite House (with large urns decorating the parapet), High Street.   CT

the Guildsmen or acquired by Guild shareholders. Braithwaite House became a hostel for the younger, unmarried men, intended to function as a kind of university hall of residence, and Ashbee and his wife, Janet, moved into Woolstaplers Hall.

As not all the Guildsmen came to Chipping Campden, and some soon returned to London, several new recruits were taken on. Among these were Fred Partridge, a jeweller from Barnstaple, Sidney Reeve, a metalworker, who had formerly worked as a schoolteacher in Worcestershire, and Alec Miller, a talented young Scottish woodcarver, who quickly won Ashbee's friendship and respect. When he arrived in Chipping Campden from the slums of Glasgow the place seemed as unreal to him as it had to Gissing twelve years before: 'I walked up Campden's one long street entranced and happy; a mile-long street with hardly a mean house, and with many of great beauty and

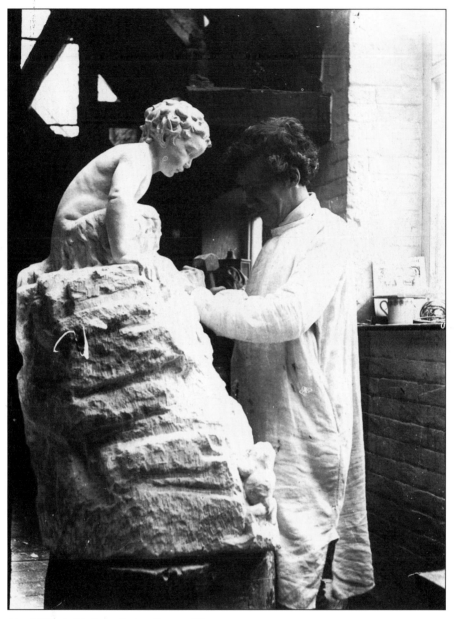

Alec Miller in his Campden studio.   CT

The silversmiths workshop. George Hart is seated second from left facing the window.   CT

richness. It was, after Glasgow and Scottish village architecture, as foreign as Cathay and as romantic as the architecture of fairy-tale illustrations. It all seemed unbelievable!'

The workshops were soon in operation, and the craftsmen generally worked a fifty hour week interspersed with regular tea-breaks when they visited each other's workshops; according to Alec Miller, this was all part of 'the widening experience'. The Guild continued to produce an extensive range of goods, including cabinet-making, wood-carving, silverwork, jewellery and forged ironwork, and commissions might vary from ornate exhibition pieces, such as inlaid furniture with elaborate metal fittings to simple, solid oak chests and bedsteads, and from intricate items of silver jewellery and church plate to sturdy metal hinges and firescreens. Among the most important commissions of this period was the decoration of the library at Madresfield Court, Worcestershire, for the seventh Earl of Beauchamp. This involved the embellishment of two new single doors and a pair of double doors with symbolic relief carvings in 1902–3, and was followed in 1905 by a commission to carve two panels eleven feet high with a Tree of Life and a Tree of Knowledge to decorate the ends of two new bookcases. The Essex

Silver chalice by the Guild.   CT

House Press was in operation by August 1902 and continued the publication of high quality specialist books that emulated the work of William Morris's Kelmscott Press. They were printed on handmade paper and illustrated with striking wood-engravings, occasionally by Ashbee himself, and bound in cream vellum or in leather with gold-tooling. A Prayer Book was produced in 1903 and a Bible was planned for the following year, together with an edition of Ashbee's own poems entitled *Echoes from the City of the Sun*.

Ashbee was very committed to the idea of creative recreation and he organized an unceasing programme of activities to keep the younger

The saw mill section of the woodworking shop. Jim Pyment can be seen in the foreground, second from left.   CT

unmarried Guildsmen happily and purposefully occupied. They put on regular plays, mainly Elizabethan dramas and concerts, and the Essex House Press even published its own songbook in 1904. There were cycling tours, and water polo and swimming parties at Westington Bathing Pool, which had been converted from the former mill pool and completed in August 1903 due to the intervention of Ashbee and Rob Martin Holland. Ashbee revelled in the local festivities, the May Day celebrations, the Whitsun wakes and the Morris dancing, and he became determined to revive Dover's Games, although this scheme met with little success. The highlight of the Guild's year was always the annual Beanfeast, and during its first summer in Chipping Campden this was organized on a much larger scale by Rob Martin Holland and held in Overbury village. There was a cricket match between the Guild and the Overbury tenants, a football match, rifle-range shooting, dancing and

Water sports at Westington Bathing Pool, *c.* 1905.   CADHAS

copious supplies of food and drink. All these activities helped to realize Ashbee's vision of English rural life, but it was a way of life very much geared towards the younger unmarried men and it probably did not occur to Ashbee to concern himself about the harsh realities of family life in a strange town. He was often away attending to business elsewhere or on lecture tours and he was fortunate that Janet was remarkably resourceful and made the best of her situation. She was only 23 when the Guild moved to Chipping Campden, almost 16 years younger than Ashbee, and their marriage was unconventional to say the least, with Janet accepted as a comrade and equal partner rather than the more usual role of the supportive wife. She was attractive, intelligent and highly perceptive, much-loved by the Guildsmen, and she took obvious delight in her mischievous and sometimes acerbic observations of Campden life. Her personal circumstances and outlandish peasant smocks may have bemused the locals, but with her open friendly manner she quickly became immensely popular with the local children, who brought her presents and trailed after her around the town. Apart from her involvement in Guild activities, she directed her energies towards local issues with great enthusiasm,

Campden School of Arts and Crafts by the
Birmingham artist, E.H. New.   BCLH

and in early 1905 she became the first woman to stand for the Campden
Rural District Council elections, although she was defeated despite a keenly
fought campaign.

The move to Chipping Campden was to provide Ashbee with the
opportunity to revive the School of Handicraft in the form of the Campden
School of Arts and Crafts. It was a fortunate coincidence that the 1902
Education Act handed the responsibility for local education from the school
boards to the county councils, and one effect of this was that grant aid
became more readily available for projects such as Ashbee had in mind. In
1904 he took over part of Elm Tree House and the disused malt-house to the
rear and converted them into a school with a gallery and library. Such was the
success of the venture that by the following year the School had 330 students
and held regular classes in various crafts, music, cookery, physical training and
gardening. During 1906 Ashbee also began to hold summer schools which
were attended by students from all over Britain, and lectures were regularly
given by such illustrious figures as Walter Crane and Patrick Geddes. Other
distinguished guests of the Ashbees included Edward Carpenter, Sidney and
Beatrice Webb, William de Morgan and also Laurence Housman and John
Masefield, who wrote a number of songs for the Essex House Songbook
extolling the delights of life in Campden. The first verse of Masefield's
'Honest Dover's Fancy' ran:

The staff of the School of Arts and Crafts. Ashbee is seated at the bottom of the steps with a little girl on his knee.   CADHAS

Campden Town
Is quiet after London riot;
Campden Street
Is kindly to the feet;
Campden wold
So bonny to behold
Is merry with the blowing wind
& glad with growing wheat.

Unfortunately the Guild workshops that sustained this admirable programme of educational and recreational activities did not flourish. In 1902 and 1903 the profits were down, and by 1904 the workshops had to be put on short time. The problems persisted, and during 1905 and 1906 the business made such a significant financial loss that a complete re-organization had to take place. The Essex House Press was closed down, the London gallery was let, a business manager was appointed to run the jewellery workshops, and the Guild was also forced to reduce its prices and produce

Physical exercises held at the rear of Elm Tree House under the watchful eye of a Volunteer officer.   CADHAS

lower quality items to attract a cheaper market. In May of the following year Ashbee made a last desperate effort to save the business and wrote to the shareholders to ask them to subscribe to a new 6 per cent Preference share, but the response was disappointing and that autumn the company was forced into liquidation. In his letter to the shareholders Ashbee had attributed the Guild's troubles to the general economic depression combined with his decision to lay off the minimum number of men, as he knew they would have problems finding work elsewhere. There was also the growing competition from large retailers like Liberty's on the one hand, and from smaller workshops and individual craftsmen with minimal overheads on the other. However it seems most likely that the move to Chipping Campden was the root cause. It was not simply the transport and communication problems, as other rural workshops managed to survive as far afield as Scotland and the West Country, and Ernest Gimson and Sidney Barnsley based in Sapperton, near Cirencester, both had full order books. But such additional costs served to exacerbate the inherent weaknesses within the Guild's administrative and financial structure, which had never fully recovered from the upheaval of the move to Campden. In 1908 the Guild of Handicraft Limited was formally wound up and many of the Guildsmen either returned to London or moved elsewhere, saddened but undoubtedly enriched by their experience. Despite

Pendant produced by the Guild.   CT

its failure Ashbee had much to be proud of, for the Guild had produced some outstanding work in a wide variety of crafts, it had trained a body of workmen and given them a better quality of life, and it had made a remarkable impact upon the people of Campden. For the work of the Guild was, in effect, the work of an entire community, and this is why Ashbee believed it still had a future.

CHAPTER FOUR

The City of the Sun

The arrival of the Guild in Chipping Campden had met with some opposition and resentment from the townspeople, and initially the relationship between the Guildsmen and the locals was strained. This was hardly surprising as, quite apart from the disruption it must have caused, the way of life, attitudes and expectations of the newcomers and the Campden people were entirely different. The situation was not helped by the eviction

T. Elsley, ironmongers, High Street.   CT

Prout's Stores. Now the Post Office and Keeley's hardware and stationery shop.   CT

of several Campden tenants by Louis Dease, who realized he could charge the Guildsmen a higher rent and make sure that urgent repair work was carried out at the same time. The local shopkeepers also took advantage and charged the Guildsmen and their families higher prices, but this probably had much to do with the low average wage of the local labourers, a mere 12s a week, compared with the wages of the Guildsmen which could vary between 30s and £4 a week. The Guildsmen and their families resented this opportunism and also grumbled to Ashbee about the lack of amenities in the town and the insanitary conditions of their living accommodation compared with the small but relatively up-to-date facilities of their London flats. Politics and religion also provided grounds for discontent. The socialist principles behind the Guild inevitably upset the local gentry, and Archie Ramage, the senior compositor, later formed a union based at the Guildsmen's club at Island

T.W. Coleman's Stores in part of Badger's Hall. Now partly used as a supermarket.   CT

A. Hartley's bakery and confectioner's shop. Now a private house.   CT

House. His strong political views upset Lord Harrowby in particular, who warned of a revolutionary element in Chipping Campden at a public meeting in Mickleton. Ashbee himself had neither the time nor the inclination for political battles, despite his strongly-held beliefs and philanthropic spirit, and he even established friendships with some the local gentry including the Redesdales from Batsford and the Dillons of Dytchley Park. Lady Elcho from Stanway was also a frequent guest of the Ashbees in Campden, often accompanied by her friend, the actress Mrs Patrick Campbell. However, the

The Campden town band, revived by Jim Pyment, *c.* 1907.   CADHAS

Ashbees never succeeded in forming a close relationship with the Earl of Gainsborough, who remained uneasy about the effect of the Guild upon the town. Religion posed a far more pressing problem. Not long after the Guild arrived, Ashbee was to receive a letter of complaint from Mrs Carrington, the vicar's wife, who had been questioning the foreman of the metal shop about the theological views of his colleagues. The vicar and his wife found the liberal attitudes of the Guildsmen particularly upsetting, and after Ashbee organized a Sunday bike ride during the Guild's first June in Chipping Campden, it became clear that he and Janet were unwelcome at the services in St James's. In 1905 the Ashbees began to attend services at Saintbury church, three and a half miles away on the other side of Dover's Hill, where they became close friends of the vicar, who had the somewhat unusual name of Muriel Nason, and they would often stay for lunch with the Nason family after the Sunday service.

During its first November in Chipping Campden the Guild invited the townspeople to co-operate with them on the arrangements for their Guy Fawkes carnival and torchlight procession. This was the first official attempt

Sign belonging to Richard Dunn, maltster and husband of Martha Dunn, who took in some of the Guildsmen as lodgers.   CT

Westington Manor, home of the Izod family.   CT

to involve the Campden people in their activities and during the following months tensions began to ease. In the New Year the Guild put on a play for the townspeople, *The New Inn* by Ben Jonson, and it was such a success it became an annual event. The two performances were packed and an additional performance was requested as well as a special matinée for the benefit of the local gentry, although the Earl of Gainsborough is said to have slept through most of the play. The plays, the processions, the concerts and outings soon became as much a part of the life of the town as of the Guild. The social club at Island House was opened to the townspeople, the village band was revived by Jim Pyment, the cabinet-maker, and the Bathing Pool became the centre of summer activities. The Guild also provided useful employment for some of the local people, notably for several masons, carpenters etc., who worked on Ashbee's architectural projects in and around the town. Others, like Mrs Martha Dunn, the bluntly-spoken but kind-hearted wife of a local maltster, virtually opened her house to the Guildsmen

Maypole dancing in the Market Square, early this century.   CT

and took in several of them as lodgers. Late in 1903 Ashbee was to describe many of the locals with considerable affection including Louis Dease, the Earl of Gainsborough's land agent, who Ashbee believed to be a compulsive liar but the lies 'were delivered with such aplomb, reveal such sympathy and versatility that it would be bad taste not to be deceived by them'. He also refers to Stanley Ulric, the Chairman of the Parish Council, 'the Rectory set', 'the lignous Grammar School master, a man very badly carved and painted', and an old spinster with a hawk-like nose and a blonde moustache, whom Charley Downer, the Guild blacksmith, had nick-named 'Old Buck Freeman'. There were also two remarkable farmer ladies, Mrs Izod from Westington, whose family had played an important role in Campden life since medieval times, and Mrs Manton, 'who came over with the Huguenot silk spinners', and two old farmers, 'Farmer Big-Shilling' who Ashbee described

Fair on Westington Green, early this century.   CT

as 'looking like a Normandy pippin, scarlet and wholesome', and 'Farmer Nibble-crust', a mercenary fellow 'like Father Christmas, with a smile of intricate benevolence'. Finally Ashbee described the 'last and most picturesque of institutions . . . old Dolphin the postman-poet, the pensioner, who keeps the childrens window and has about 15 hats that he wreathes around with flowers. He walks along the street with a kitten on his shoulder. Old Dolphin has a sense of beauty and we love him for it.'

Quite apart from the new range of activities introduced into the town by the Guild, Chipping Campden also began to benefit from a number of cultured and artistic new visitors and residents, many of whom were drawn to the town by the Guild's reputation or were simply attracted by its unspoilt character and rich folk and craft traditions. In 1902, the same year as the Guild came to Chipping Campden, the Chelsea artist George Loosely settled in the town. Ashbee converted a barn into a studio for him in Calf's Lane and

Loosely later married the statuesque Statia Power, the Guild bookbinder. He was followed in 1904 by the etcher and draughtsman, F.L. Griggs (1876–1938), a youthful but rather earnest young man of strong principle and with a very generous nature. Griggs had been articled to the architect C.E. Mallows in 1896, but abandoned architecture to work as an artist and illustrator two years later and soon acquired a reputation for his topographical scenes and imaginary medieval landscapes. He was preparing drawings for the Oxfordshire and Cotswolds volume of Macmillan's *Highways and Byways* series when he first arrived in Chipping Campden on his Rex motor tricycle, and was so captivated by the place that he decided to stay permanently. He lodged at Braithwaite House till 1905 and then took out a lease on Dover's House, which was to remain his home until 1927. He initially furnished the house with fine Georgian furniture and silver but, according to Alec Miller, his tastes grew simpler and less sophisticated as he settled into rural life and around 1920 the house was 'all furnished with furniture of Gimson's raw oak and iron candlesticks replace his Sheffield plate ones . . . '. Griggs found the hectic, intellectual and rather élitist lifestyle of the Ashbees ill-suited to his temperament, and he was to become a close friend of the Sapperton craftsmen with whom he shared a deep joy in the small details and simple pleasures of country life. For a brief period before Gimson's death in 1919, Griggs even set up an architectural partnership with him. It is interesting that before Griggs became friends with Gimson and the Barnsley brothers there was virtually no contact between the two craft communities, despite their common interest in the life and work of Morris and the ethos of his teaching. This was most probably due to their differences in personality and attitude, but it also reflects the individualism that was prevalent within the Arts and Crafts Movement. In 1930 Griggs moved to Dover's Court in Back Ends, a house he built for himself between 1927 and 1938 in a traditional style that adhered closely to Arts and Crafts principles, with interior fittings and furnishings by Cotswold craftsmen. After he became a Catholic in 1912, he was welcomed into the local Catholic community, and many years later, in 1935, he designed a new priest's house adjacent to the Catholic church. However, his major contribution to Chipping Campden was to be the prominent role he played in the conservation of the town between the Wars.

Another artist and devout Catholic who settled in the town at this time was Paul Woodroffe (1875–1945), the book illustrator and stained glass artist, a tall, beady-eyed man of austere habits, whom Janet Ashbee nick-named 'Bête-Grise'. He established a workshop at his house in Westington, which Ashbee repaired and extended for him, and he was to design two windows for the Catholic church in Campden, one between 1905 and 1907, the other in 1930.

Dover's House, High Street.   CT

View down the road into Campden from Paul Woodroffe's House.   CT

By 1906 the lives of the Guildsmen and the townspeople were quite interwoven, many of the Guildsmen had married local girls and the Guild's social calendar had become part of the pattern of life in Campden. Early that year Janet was to write:

Nearly 4 years in this little grey City – it seems more like 40! The weather-worn dove coloured stone has a way of catching and fixing one's affections; and even the opposition, the Vicar, the pig-headed farmers, the stupid politicians . . . are all part of it – and seem as necessary as the mist and the rain and the rheumatism and the muddy roads, – yes and the Sundays over Dover's Hill to Saintbury, the hockey matches, the swimming lake and the Xmas play.

That summer the renewed sense of confidence and purpose which pulsed within the town was reflected by the elaborate celebrations to mark the coming of age of Viscount Campden, the son of the Earl of Gainsborough, the focus of which was a large garden party held on the lawn at Campden House. According to the *Evesham Journal*:

> Refreshments were dispensed from a buffet table erected in a large marquee, and this was supported by numerous small tables placed about the lawn, and on the terraces in the shadow of the trees. There was a lavish display of high-class confectionery, strawberries and cream, pines, melons, ices and so on . . . In the park adjoining the mansion were free roundabouts and swings, coconut shies, a shooting gallery, and other amusements of the same sort for the delectation of the young.

However, it was significant that the rigid class structure still retained its grip upon the town despite the liberal attitudes of many of its new inhabitants, for Ashbee was to observe that there was not a single labourer present at this lavish reception – although his social conscience does not seem to have prevented him from accepting his own invitation.

The following year life in Chipping Campden was further enriched by the arrival of three new inhabitants. The first of these was Wentworth Huyshe, stepfather to the Hart brothers, George and Will, the Guild silversmith and woodcarver, both of whom had been with Ashbee since the Guild's London days. Huyshe had worked as a war correspondent and was also an enthusiastic amateur historian and a great raconteur, much to the delight of the young men at Braithwaite House where he first took lodgings. He eventually moved to Broad Campden, where he worked as a heraldic artist, and his son, Reynell later shared a workshop with his stepbrother George.

Another new resident of Broad Campden was Ananda Coomaraswamy, a mineralogist and leading authority on Indian life and religion, whose wife Ethel was the sister of Fred Partridge, the Guild jeweller. In 1905 Coomaraswamy had asked Ashbee to restore and extend the Norman chapel in Broad Campden for him, a project Ashbee had been eager to undertake since 1903. The Coomaraswamys moved in to the chapel in 1907, and they soon became good friends of the Ashbees, acquired shares in the Guild, and even took over the Essex House Press until 1910 so that Coomaraswamy could publish a number of his own works as well as some of Ashbee's. The Coomaraswamys must have appeared a strange, exotic couple even to the people of Campden, who had become accustomed to the unusual habits and appearance of its new residents. According to Janet Ashbee, 'Both of them lived in their enchanted chapel, which glows rose colour with linen and Morris hangings and Oriental crimsons, like two elves, creatures you cannot gossip with, and that yet have something more human about them than the

Interior of the Norman Chapel, Broad Campden, showing the study area at the east end of the library.   · CT

most ordinary of us.' The Norman chapel briefly became a focal point of cultural activities in the area and visitors included the artist William Rothenstein, who had moved to Oakridge Lynch in 1910, and his friend, the Indian philosopher, Rabindranath Tagore. Coomaraswamy's view of art was deeply rooted in his spiritual beliefs and far removed from Ashbee's Ruskinian belief in its social purpose, but was to become an important influence on the work of Eric Gill. After the Coomaraswamys left Chipping Campden in 1911, they let the chapel to the Ashbees, who were to remain there in considerable contentment till 1919.

The third new resident of Chipping Campden was Philippe Mairet, who came to work as a draughtsman in Ashbee's architectural office on the recommendation of his headmaster – who happened to be the father of George Chettle, Ashbee's architectural assistant. Mairet threw himself into

Thatched cottage with family and neighbours.   CT

Guild life with great enthusiasm, his talents flourished and he was later to become an accomplished illustrator, writer, actor and stained glass artist. Ethel Coomaraswamy obviously found his charms irresistible and left her husband and moved to Sussex with Mairet. There she established a workshop in Ditchling and became an important figure in the revival of English hand-weaving.

Thus, by the time the Guild had disbanded in 1908, the structure of the local community had already begun to change significantly and so the town was not as badly affected as it might have been. It was beginning to attract an increasing number of tourists which was bringing in a welcome new source of income, and its educational and cultural resources were attracting attention from all over Britain. In many ways the town had actually outgrown the Guild and this was true of many of the Guildsmen too, for many had adjusted to their new surroundings so well that even Ashbee came to realize they could now survive on their own. As he was later to admit: 'They had captured the countryside, they had got the confidence of the farmers, they had made friends, many had found their wives locally, they had in fact made a new country life, and another generation was at hand.' Furthermore, all this had been achieved without any loss to the historic character of the town. On the contrary, Ashbee's architectural work was visible proof of the town's revival and its new sense of identity.

CHAPTER FIVE

Rebuilding Utopia

Although much of Ashbee's time was taken up by his role as director and designer of the Guild of Handicraft, he was an architect by profession and the architectural offices he maintained at Elm Tree House and in London formed a very important aspect of his work. Like many of his fellow architects within the Arts and Crafts Movement he believed that architecture made possible the true unity of the arts, as an appropriate setting for mural painting, plasterwork, furniture, textiles etc., and provided a means of expressing his ideas on the important role of crafts in society, his respect for tradition, his desire to improve the living and working environment and the important role of nature in the design process. Most Arts and Crafts architects shared an appreciation of vernacular building, and the buildings of the Cotswold region attracted particular attention, largely due to the influence of William Morris. One of the first young architects to visit Chipping Campden was the Glasgow Arts and Crafts architect C.R. Mackintosh, who came to the town in 1894 on his first sketching tour outside Scotland. Most of the sketches he made are of windows, doorways and woodwork, and he seems to have been especially interested in the patterns of leaded glass and tracery rather than in the buildings themselves. Several Arts and Crafts architects and craftsmen worked in the area around the turn of the century, including Guy Dawber, C.E. Bateman and Ernest Newton and some, like Ernest Gimson, Sidney and Ernest Barnsley, and Ashbee himself, actually settled in the area. All were to contribute to the growing interest in traditional Cotswold building and an understanding of its repair and conservation.

In general Ashbee's architectural work varied from the stylish sophistication of his town houses in Cheyne Walk, Chelsea, to the simple, roughcast country cottages he designed with a view to economy and practicality. However, his work in Chipping Campden reveals an admirable appreciation of traditional building materials and methods and is very much in sympathy with its surroundings. At Elm Tree House he had two assistants, the occasional pupil and a lady secretary, who dutifully commuted to London with him, and, up till 1906, the office was kept reasonably busy with conversion and alteration work. In 1906 Ashbee published *A Book of Cottages and Little Houses: for Landlords, Architects, Builders and Others*, which described

Izod's Cottage, Park Road of 1902 by
C.R. Ashbee. Drawn by F.L. Griggs in
1905.   BCLH

much of his work in Chipping Campden to illustrate his views on the ethics,
aesthetics and economics of building in the country, a subject of
contemporary popular debate due in part to the growing popularity of the
garden city movement. In this book he was to claim that 'no one can really
build well in the country who has not to start with some love for landscape,
for colour, for wind, rain, and sunshine; for the open air.' To this he might
have added that no one can build really well in Chipping Campden High
Street without some knowledge of the local building materials and practices,
in particular, the characteristics of the Cotswold style such as the tall gables,
steep roof pitch (usually around 55 degrees) and mullioned windows, the
sense of scale and proportion and the restrained but infinite variety of detail
achieved by the Cotswold masons.

Among the first projects he undertook was the rebuilding of Izod's Cottage
in Park Road, a pair of cottages that belonged to Mr William Nathan Izod of
the local farming family. The cottage was constructed with materials salvaged
from the site and, as Ashbee noted in *A Book of Cottages and Little Houses*:
'The stones were very carefully coursed so as to assist the rather subtle
proportions aimed at, & the roofing slatts were similarly laid in gradation –
the larger and heavier at the eaves, the smaller near the ridge.' He was to add

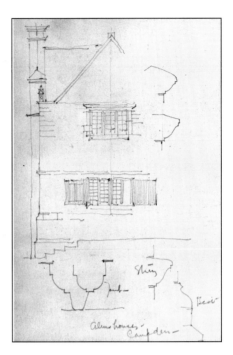

The Almshouses, Chipping Campden.
Sketched by C.R. Mackintosh in 1894.
Hunterian Art Gallery, University of Glasgow

that the 'beauty of old masonry and roofing lies in observing details of this kind.' Other important features of the design are the steep pitch of the roof, the tall chimneys, the carefully-spaced, ground-floor mullioned windows, the dormer windows, and the position of the doorway to the left of centre for practical reasons and visual effect. Inside the house the inglenook fireplaces from the former two cottages were incorporated into the hall and parlour, and four small bedrooms were created upstairs, the plan being determined by the width of the building and the size of the garden. The success of the design is evident from the street elevation as it is difficult to believe that it was only built early this century. Compared with Daintree further along the street, a house built during the same year by local builders according to Ashbee's general instructions, it becomes clear that the instinctive feel for detail and proportion for which the Cotswold masons are renowned had suffered since the demise of the Cotswold style in the late seventeenth century. Ashbee was also aware of the unsatisfactory result and believed that the plan had not been considered in proper relation to the elevation, the dormers were too large and too high, the timbers were too thin and 'what purport to be leaded lights are cast iron facsimiles.'

In 1903 Ashbee rebuilt High House in Sheep Street, a cottage leased to the Guildsmen from the Earl of Gainsborough. Again materials were salvaged

Forge Cottages on the western outskirts of the town, now demolished. Typical example of a thatched building in the Cotswold style.   CT

from the site, and the ground floor of the former cottage was retained as a basement, an ingenious device that had the practical advantage of damp-proofing the building as well as making it appear larger and more impressive from the street. Two sets of drawings were made, the earlier of June 1902 for Bill Thornton, the later of October 1903 for Archie Ramage, which vary with regard to the type of lintels proposed and the size of the windows. A compromise was reached in the final scheme, and although the small casements, lean-to porch and minimal detail make no concession to prettiness the charm of the building lies in its simplicity, solidity and its tall, distinctive profile which has now become an important feature of this narrow street.

Also during 1903 Ashbee carried out essential repairs to the south-east pier of the Market Hall which was suffering from damage and erosion, and he converted a house, Brooklyn, in Park Road for Rob Martin Holland to provide additional accommodation for the Guild. The building was gutted, the doors were removed at the front and side, windows were inserted, the eaves were raised and the building was re-roofed with thatch. Ashbee, like many other Arts and Crafts architects, was very enthusiastic about thatching due to its textural appeal, the organic qualities it gave to a building as well as its value as a rural craft. 'A close observation of the work of a first-rate

Block of four cottages at Catbrook of 1903 by C.R. Ashbee, photographed just after they had been completed.   CT

thatcher is very instructive: he works instinctively in line and mass together. Every little break or stepping in the wall face is an opportunity, and the diminishing curve of a projection is to him a chance of producing forms peculiar to his material, & forms often very beautiful indeed . . .'

However, despite his undoubted interest and understanding of the local building traditions, Ashbee was equally capable of defying these for reasons of social and economic necessity. At Catbrook, on the outskirts of Chipping Campden, he designed several blocks of three-bedroomed labourers cottages between 1902 and 1905, two of which were built. The first of these, Maryvale and Catbrook Furlong, are semi-detached, and were built for a Mr J. Bell Gripper in 1902–3; the second comprised a block of four cottages, Clapgat, Greenstead, The Haven and Paynsley, built in 1903 on land owned by Ashbee. Both are constructed of roughcast stock brick, partly because it was relatively cheap and also because Ashbee liked its lack of pretension and ability to blend with any surroundings. Only the semi-detached block was given a stone slate roof, stone chimneys and stone dressings; the larger block had a thatched roof, since replaced with machine-tiles much to the detriment of its appearance, and brick chimneys with stone caps. The simple, timber casement windows were brought flush with the wall surface to heighten the

Rear of Woolstaplers Hall.   CT

appearance of solidity, and the steeply-pitched roofs help to lessen the bulk of both buildings. Ashbee's aim was to design cheap housing that resembled a cottage as opposed to a villa with a bay window 'calculated to hold a table eighteen inches square, upon which is a machine-crocheted cloth and a vase of wax flowers, or some other useless ornament'. As each block only cost around £900 to build, including their neat gardens, he certainly achieved this, but despite his good intentions the houses inevitably looked a little bland compared with the sturdy grey-gold houses nearby.

Between 1902 and 1904 Ashbee also converted several important buildings in the town for the use of the Guild, including the old silk mill, Braithwaite House, Island House and Elm Tree House, but none of them required any significant alteration to the exterior, with the possible exception of Elm Tree House where Ashbee had to replace some openings in the front and rear elevations. His plans for the fourteenth-century Woolstaplers Hall were intended to be far more extensive but were only executed in part due to the uncertainty surrounding the Guild's future. When the Ashbees moved into the building it was, according to Ashbee, 'known as "The Hollies" or "The Laurels" or some equally pointless suburban name', and since the eighteenth century it had suffered from several unsympathetic alterations, including the addition of a nineteenth-century bay window beneath the oriel window in the front elevation, and internal work that had concealed the medieval roof structure beneath a layer of plaster and whitewash and had partially chopped away and blocked the carved stone fireplace. Ashbee uncovered the fine oak roof and a medieval traceried archway and also repaired the fireplace as best he could. In doing so he made the interesting discovery that this main first-floor room was once reached by an external staircase and had a two-light window that looked out towards the church. The room became the Ashbees' library, and it was filled with their fine collection of Oriental rugs, oak furniture, copper clocks, silver dishes, William Morris curtains and, of course, Ashbee's outstanding collection of books. Alec Miller was to remember it as something 'unique and beautiful; the books, perhaps six or seven thousand of them, were to me a constant source of delight', and it was to become a favourite meeting-place among the Guildsmen, who held their regular Friday night sing-songs there. Between 1907 and 1909 Ashbee made plans for a more ambitious scheme of alteration. The alterations to the front elevation had obscured all traces of the original entrance, but some stones that were dug up in the garden seemed to suggest that it was once formed by an early Perpendicular arch. Ashbee designed a new entrance beneath the oriel, the keystone of which was intended to have a woolstapler on it carved by Alec Miller, and he also made plans for the demolition of part of the south range, which was to be adapted as a service wing, and the addition of substantial extensions to the rear of the main building to provide a hall and music room. This new layout would incorporate both a kitchen court and a new formal garden with rectangular beds, pergolas and a long vista leading to a pear tree. However only the new entrance was actually executed as Ashbee became distracted by the Guild's problems, but it probably would have been one of his most interesting architectural projects not just in Campden but of his entire career.

After 1904 Ashbee became less preoccupied with small-scale design jobs on behalf of the Guild and, apart from the conversion of Elm Tree House, a few more unexecuted designs for buildings at Catbrook and his plans for Woolstaplers Hall, his architectural work in Chipping Campden was confined to two commissions in Westington and the conversion of the Norman chapel in Broad Campden.

One of the Westington projects involved making primarily cosmetic alterations to The Cedars (now Abbotsbury) for the playwright, St John Hankin, who had moved there from the new Bedford Park estate in London in 1905. The other Westington commission revealed a more inventive and confident adaptation of the local building traditions than Ashbee had hitherto attempted. In 1904 he was asked by Paul Woodroffe, the stained glass artist, to repair and remodel a derelict thatched cottage (now called Woodroffe House) adjacent to the house of his brother-in-law, Joseph Moorat. The building was in a very dilapidated condition and Ashbee had to re-thatch the roof, re-glaze the windows, install a damp course and open up the former inglenook fireplace. He also built an addition with an asymmetric gable onto the front elevation to house a new entrance hall and staircase with a bathroom above, and this was skilfully designed so as to appear part of the original building, enhance the rather mundane appearance of the former front elevation and make the most of its prominent situation at the upper end of the main street. A more curious and surprising feature of Ashbee's scheme was the re-facing of the service wing with white matt-glazed bricks, but Ashbee does not give any reason for this unusual choice of material in his book. He also converted the former stable into a studio complete with a separate kiln room and cutting-room for Woodroffe's stained glass work.

Ashbee's conversion of the Norman chapel was to be his major architectural achievement in and around Chipping Campden. When he began work on the building in 1905 it was completely derelict and the chancel had been demolished, although it still retained much of its fifteenth-century alterations when a floor had been inserted in the nave and an addition built on at the west end to enable the building to be used as a dwelling. Ashbee's initial plans were to add a small hall with a staircase on the site of the former chancel, with a wing running south to provide a music room and bedrooms. This would have obscured part of the south wall and fortunately a more successful solution was found whereby the chancel arch was used as a large window to light a music room on the ground floor of the nave, and a library was situated above with a study area at its eastern end where the floor level was slightly raised above the chancel arch. Part of the nave walls had to be rebuilt and buttressed and a long run of leaded casements were inserted to light the study area on the first floor. A dining-room, hallway and two first-floor bedrooms were situated in the fifteenth-century addition and a new, two-storey, oak bay window with roughcast spandrels was added to provide extra light. At the north-west end a new service wing was built on, constructed from roughcast brick with white-painted timber, a simple and unpretentious addition that visually could neither compete with, nor detract from the main building. Thus, the completed scheme was an admirable example of the principles recommended by Morris's Society for the Protection of Ancient Buildings as it was a practical and workable solution that neither masked nor altered the character and scale of the original building. Ashbee was fortunate that Coomaraswamy proved a very sympathetic client, equally unconstrained by convention and with similar

The Norman Chapel, Broad Campden, just after Ashbee had restored and converted it in
1906.   CT

tastes in interior decoration. The library of the chapel glowed with rich
textiles, and with its simple oak furniture, including a fine trestle table from
the workshop of A. Rowney Green, must have appeared very similar to
Ashbee's own library at Woolstaplers Hall.

These architectural projects in Campden certainly provided Ashbee with
ample opportunity to demonstrate to the local people how their historic
buildings could best be adapted to modern use without loss to their individual
character or the fabric of the town. It was a message that Campden could not
afford to ignore in the coming decades.

CHAPTER SIX

The Legacy of the Guild

After the Guild went into liquidation several of the Guildsmen chose to stay on in Chipping Campden and continued to work at the silk mill under their own names. Among them were Alec Miller and Will Hart, the sculptors and carvers, Charley Downer and Bill Thornton the blacksmiths, and George Hart the silversmith. The mill itself was bought by Jim Pyment, who had been the foreman of the cabinet-making shop, and he started up a building firm, J.W. Pyment & Sons, which was to be responsible for much of the high quality traditional building work undertaken in the area over the coming years.

Ashbee never lost sight of his original aim to establish a co-operative craft community in rural surroundings, and in 1908 he published a book in support of his ideas entitled *Craftsmanship in Competitive Industry*. In the book he argued for effective legislation to sustain the crafts and also for trade-unionism, although he still held fast to his belief that craftsmanship and husbandry could form a worthwhile partnership. In 1904 he had visited the Whiteway settlement, near Miserden, Gloucestershire, a self-supporting community of Tolstoyan anarchists, who led a Spartan existence living off the produce of an infertile 40-acre site. Ashbee admired their pioneering spirit but he considered their lifestyle to be too 'uncouth and experimental' for his tastes. In 1908 he began negotiations with Joseph Fels, the American naptha soap millionaire and a keen supporter of the 'Back-to-the-Land' movement, which led to the formation of the Guild of Handicraft Trust, a fairly informal association between the remaining Guildsmen, Ashbee and Fels. In 1909 Fels purchased 75 acres of land at Broad Campden on behalf of the Trust upon which the Guildsmen were to establish smallholdings. However, only George Hart, already an experienced farmer, was to make a success of the scheme, and the Trust became increasingly inactive and was finally closed down altogether in 1919. By that time the Ashbees and their four daughters had left Chipping Campden for good and moved to Jerusalem, where Ashbee had been appointed Civic Advisor to the British Military Government.

Till the outbreak of the First World War life in Chipping Campden continued much as usual. The market was still held on the last Wednesday of the month, with the sheep held in pens in the Square and the cattle and pigs

The sheep market in the Market Square, *c.* 1910.   CT

kept in a paddock to the rear of the Noel Arms. In 1904 the town had benefited from its first piped water supply, and the local doctor had acquired Campden's first motor car, a tiller-steered Stanley steam car, but these were the only signs of the changes to come. After the Guild went into liquidation, visitors continued to call upon the Ashbees and see around the silk mill workshops, and the School of Arts and Crafts managed to attract a steady flow of students till it eventually closed in 1916. There was even a royal visit in May 1908, when Edward VII passed through the town during a brief stay with the Redesdales at Batsford Park. Bob Dickenson, a local newspaper seller, was quick to take advantage of this event, and stopped the royal car in Broad Campden to sell the King a newspaper. He then painted a version of the royal arms on his canvas bag and claimed to be a purveyor to royalty. It is not known whether his trade increased thereafter. Other notable visitors to the town during this period included the American architect, Frank Lloyd Wright. Ashbee had met him in Chicago in December 1900 while on a lecture tour sponsored by the National Trust, and Wright arrived in Chipping Campden in 1910 eager to meet Ashbee again on his home ground. The town also continued to attract unconventional new residents, among them the

Edward VII's visit to the town in 1908.   CT

Blanco-Whites, who moved into Island House in 1913. Mrs Amber Blanco-White was the heroine of H.G. Wells' *Anne Veronica* and *The New Machiavelli* and was also reputed to be the mother of his child, a scandal which sustained Campden gossip for several months.

After August 1914 this pattern of life began to slowly disintegrate. Most of the young men of Campden left to serve in the Gloucestershire Regiment under the command of Viscount Campden, while others joined the Warwickshire Yeomanry, many of them young farmers' sons using their own horses, or the Volunteers. Even if Ashbee's Guild had prospered it would undoubtedly have been torn apart by the war. Sixty-two Campden men were killed, a grim total of one in five of their age group. An elegant memorial was designed by Griggs to stand on a site between the Market Hall and the Town Hall in an attractive landscaped setting, but although it now seems so much a part of the town centre, the scheme divided the community. Many local people believed it inappropriate for the memorial to be designed by a member of the Roman Catholic Church and the row persisted for more than

War Memorial by F.L. Griggs taken soon after it was erected in 1920.   CT

eighteen months until finally a town meeting voted in favour of Griggs's proposal. Despite the opposition he met with in Campden, Griggs was also to design many memorials in other Cotswold towns and villages, including Broadway, Blockley, Biddenham, Chedworth, Painswick, Snowshill, Weston-sub-Edge, Winchcombe and Willersley and these were accepted more graciously by the local residents. Henry Payne of Amberley also designed a memorial window in the east end of the parish church, and both this and Griggs's memorial were to bear witness to not only the resilience of the Campden people but also the town's reputation as a centre of the crafts.

During the war years, in the Easter of 1916, there was an unusually heavy fall of snow in Campden, and with most of the young men away it was up to the older residents to clear the streets and try and open up the routes to the neighbouring towns and villages. Apparently one day during the Great Snow, several men were gathered in a shop in Leysbourne huddled around a closed fire that was giving out very little heat. A certain Bob Coldicot claimed he knew an excellent means of solving the problem and disappeared to the local chemist. At this time the chemists used to keep small stocks of gunpowder, and Coldicot returned with a small packet of the stuff tucked under his arm.

The Great Snow of 1916. Notice the absence of young men helping with the clearing of snow.
CADHAS

One of the men, Harry Blake, cast the gunpowder into the fire and held the lid down. It exploded within seconds with such force that it blasted the chimney off the top of the roof. The flying debris narrowly missed a farmer, Bill Hayes, who was walking down the road with a basket of eggs carried on his head which he hoped to send by carrier to Stratford market. The eggs were all broken, the snow was black with soot in every direction, and Hayes was lucky to escape with his life.

The resilence of the Campden people was to prove a considerable asset during the inter-war years. Among the first important changes that were to occur was the break up of the Gainsborough estate to pay the death duties that resulted from the successive deaths of the third and fourth Earls. However, despite the ripples this created within Campden society, the sale of Campden House was to have beneficial consequences as the new owners commissioned Norman Jewson, Gimson's former architectural assistant and a close friend of Griggs, to carry out a sensitive scheme of restoration on the building. Griggs collaborated with Jewson on the project, which involved the removal of some of R.C. Carpenter's ill-proportioned additions, including a large service range which was replaced by a new terrace and summerhouse. Less welcome were the council houses which sprang up along the Aston Road to provide homes for the soldiers who returned to Chipping Campden, and later appeared around the outskirts of the town on the small estates at Berrington, Broad Campden, Catbrook and Littleworth. Admittedly they fulfilled an important need as the housing shortage was acute, but many paid insufficient regard to the local building traditions. Although Campden had had a piped water supply since 1904, the other essential services of modern life took a little longer to arrive. It was not until 1923 that the town was provided with a telephone link, and 1926 that a sewerage scheme was started; previously, many of the smaller cottages in the alleys leading off the main streets had been forced to share an earth closet. In 1928 the town was at last connected to the mains electricity supply, twenty-six years after an electric power plant had first been installed at the silk mill by Ashbee. During 1926 many of the people in the town were also to welcome the arrival of the first motor bus, which provided a useful link with other towns in the area such as Evesham and thus enabled many of the local young people to seek employment further afield while still remaining residents of Chipping Campden.

The agricultural depression gradually lessened its grip, and by the 1920s tractors and other forms of agricultural machinery had begun to replace both the horse and the steam engine in the fields and contributed much to the efficiency of the more prosperous farms that could afford them. Ironically, the modernization of the local farms was to coincide with a brief revival of the wool trade, and sales of wool were held in a barn not far from the parish church. However, by the 1930s this trade had dwindled to an insignificant amount and its demise was closely followed by the disappearance of the monthly sheep market in the town square. The Square, like so many others of its kind, has since been converted into a car park. Although many of Campden's small industrial operations, such as the silk mill and the rope and sack works, had ceased production by the end of the nineteenth century, some were more successful and basket-making certainly continued well into the 1920s. One local man, a Mr H. Ellis, employed five or six men at this time to make fruit baskets to supply the market gardeners in the Evesham Vale. A new and more successful enterprise also became established at the mill buildings adjoining the railway station. Before the First World War the buildings had housed Clark's pheasant farm and poultry and dog food business, which, at the height of its prosperity, claimed to produce two thousand pheasant eggs a day. In 1919 this became the Campden Research Station for the study of food preservation methods, and among its many contributions in this field it has been responsible for the introduction of Campden tablets, commonly used in home wine-making and brewing.

The North Cotswold Hunt in the Market Square.   CT

One notable survivor of Chipping Campden's traditional way of life was the North Cotswold Hunt. Since the mid-eighteenth century the town had established a reputation as a fox-hunting centre, and since the formation of the North Cotswold Hunt in 1868 the regular meets had become an important and profitable part of the life of the town. During the 1920s there were still five blacksmiths shops in Campden and ten years later houses continued to be rented and hotels filled for the hunting.

More significantly, Chipping Campden maintained its reputation as a centre of the arts and crafts, and between the Wars artists, writers, scholars and craftsmen continued to come to Campden to live and work, including Graham Greene, Leo and Eileen Baker, W.K. Hudson and the Birmingham jewellers Bernard Sleigh and Arthur and Georgie Gaskin. In 1928 H.P.R. Finberg moved to Campden and set up the Alcuin Press at Elm Tree House, following the example of Ashbee's Essex House Press. Finberg was the son of A.J. Finberg, the biographer of J.M.W. Turner, and his mother ran a gallery in London that specialized in work by Cotswold artists and craftsmen. The Alcuin Press only lasted till the mid-1930s but published several notable works including A.E. Housman's poems and Cavendish's *Life of Wolsey*. Another new resident was Sir Gordon Russell. Since his father, S.B. Russell, had taken over the Lygon Arms in Broadway in 1904, Gordon Russell had developed a deep love of the Cotswold countryside and its craft traditions. As a boy he had been educated at the Grammar School in Chipping Campden and had later attended life classes at the Campden School of Arts and Crafts so was quite familiar with the Campden community from an early age. Despite the rapid development of his furniture business and, later, the public duties that occupied an increasing proportion of his time, he maintained his close links with the area and in 1924 he bought a field up on Dover's Hill and asked the architect Leslie Mansfield to design a house for him. 'Kingcombe', as the house was called, was completed in 1926, employing local labour, and was a striking combination of traditional and contemporary influences. Russell was to spend much of his free time there creating a beautiful and unusual garden based on a plan drawn up for him in the 1930s by Geoffrey Jellicoe.

Many distinguished visitors came to Chipping Campden to call upon F.L. Griggs, such as Sir Alfred Munnings, Graham Sutherland, Gilbert Spence, T.S. Eliot and Paul and John Nash. This helped to sustain the town's artistic reputation and in 1924, as a tribute to Ashbee's endeavours, Griggs founded the Campden Society, its aims being to protect the beauty and character of the town, preserve its ancient crafts and traditions and promote its reputation as an art centre. Regular Arts and Crafts exhibitions were held, but Griggs soon became frustrated with the Society as it failed to consult him on major issues and he was to resign in 1927. Two years later he founded the Campden Trust, a small limited company that took over the Campden Society's work of protecting the town's buildings from inappropriate development and which sought to maintain the standards of design and conservation that Ashbee had established. As tourism and the technological advances of the twentieth century began to threaten the town's historic character this work was to occupy an increasing proportion of Griggs's time and energy. It often appeared a thankless task and he was frequently criticized for obstructing the path of progress, but with hindsight we can now recognize the true significance of his contribution.

CHAPTER SEVEN

The Conservation of Campden

F.L. Griggs had a profound love for the English countryside and its traditions that went far deeper than Ashbee's romantic but rather detached vision of rural life. He derived great contentment from the rhythm of the seasons, the lambing, the harvest, the rituals, festivals and holidays, and took delight in the simplest of pleasures, such as the birdsong, the wild flowers and the hedgerows. This love is implicit in his etchings of rural scenes, both real and imaginary, their technical virtuosity of detail often overwhelmed by the contrasts of light and shade that exude a sense of deep tranquillity and innocence. However much of his work is also filled with an air of melancholy that reveals Griggs's deep sense of loss as he witnessed the disintegration of the society and traditions that he cherished. He was an ardent supporter of the emerging conservation movement, a member of both the Society for the Protection of Ancient Buildings and the Council for the Preservation of Rural England, and he was to derive inspiration from the writings of Ruskin, Morris and leading Arts and Crafts theorists, such as W.R. Lethaby, who had published his influential book *Form in Civilisation* in 1922.

Chipping Campden seemed to Griggs to be the epitome of everything he loved about English rural life. The peal of eight bells in St James's church was one of his greatest joys and he was to institute an annual bell-ringers feast at the Lygon Arms, where a traditional and hearty menu of roast beef, apple pie and cream and English cheeses was consumed amidst much good-humoured banter, assisted by generous supplies of best draught ale from Stratford. During the 1920s Griggs used his growing reputation as an artist to the benefit of the town, but his concern and generosity were to place immense strain upon his health and his personal finances. In 1923 he used this influence to persuade the Post Office to lay the telephone cables underground and to use grey paint instead of red on the public call-boxes. In 1928 he achieved a similar success with the Shropshire, Worcestershire and Staffordshire Electric Company, although many of the small gas lanterns which Griggs designed for the town, said to have produced a jewel-like effect at night, were either scrapped or sold once the electricity supply had been installed. A major achievement of this period was his successful campaign to save Dover's Hill from development. In 1926 the Earl of Harrowby decided to

View of St James's church before Griggs's gas lanterns were removed.   CADHAS

sell 950 acres of his estate, part of which included Dover's Hill, and a hotel was proposed as a suitable use for the site. Griggs risked everything he possessed by putting forward a bid of £4,400 to buy Dover's Hill, hopefully as a temporary measure till the money could be raised to pass it on to the National Trust. The bid was accepted but, despite national appeals for money by the Trust in *The Times* and elsewhere, support was slow in coming and Griggs was obliged to write a personal cheque for £2,000 in the meantime. Eventually many of his wealthy friends came to his rescue and Dover's Hill was finally conveyed to the National Trust in December 1928. However, although Griggs's efforts were widely applauded in the national and local press, the people of Campden do not appear to have shown Griggs the gratitude he truly deserved.

When the Campden Trust was founded in 1929, Griggs may well have hoped that he would be able to share the burden of safeguarding the historic fabric of the town from further unsympathetic development. However, although his close friend and colleague Norman Jewson and other committee members such as Ben Chandler of Hidcote, Sir Philip Stott of Stanton and William Cadbury played a valuable role in the administration of the Trust's work, Griggs still seems to have shouldered most of the responsibility. During the first years of the Trust's life a number of properties were bought and restored by Griggs and Jewson, including the Old King's Arms, the Old

The Old King's Arms after Griggs and
Jewson restored it in 1929.   CT

Plough Inn (now Robert Welch's showrooms) and Elsley House, south of the
Town Hall, primarily with funds provided by Sir Philip Stott and William
Cadbury. Many of the fine wrought iron hanging signs in the town were also
designed by Griggs and installed at this time. Less satisfactory were the events
of 1931 when the local council put forward a proposal to construct eight red
brick houses along Station Road. Griggs was appalled at the prospect but to
build in stone would have cost an extra £80 per house. Eventually he
managed to persuade the Council to use roughcast and lime-wash on the
houses and incorporate stone quoins into their design, thus reducing their
impact and also the extra costs to only £428, £200 of which was paid by the
Campden Trust and the remainder raised by individual contributions. This
was to set an important precedent, and the majority of council houses built in
the town since, in Littleworth, Berrington and Catbrook for example, may
lack the fine proportions and detailing of Campden's older buildings, but
most have been constructed from reconstituted local stone. Although this
does not weather to the subtle colours of unprocessed material, it is much less
intrusive than red brick and increased demand for the product has provided
several local quarries with sufficient work to continue in operation.

The following year yet another victory was won when Griggs succeeded in
preventing the County Council from destroying the broad grass verges which

Dover's Court under construction, *c.* 1930.   CT

contribute so much to the character of the town centre, and two other major successes were achieved by the Campden Trust in the following years. The first of these occurred in 1934 when it bought the Coneygree, an area of open land adjacent to the parish church and the ruins of Sir Baptist Hicks's Campden House, for the sum of £1,500 and handed it over to the National Trust. Then in 1942 the Trust also arranged the purchase of the seventeenth-century Market Hall for £275 from the Noel family, largely due to the generosity of William Cadbury. At the time it was threatened with demolition and removal to the United States and it was not without some relief that this major feature of the town centre was transferred to the National Trust.

Between 1927 and 1938 Griggs worked on Dover's House in Back Ends, which he designed for himself and his growing family to set an example of good design and sound craftsmanship. However his exacting standards and the crippling financial costs of the project caused endless frustration and worry and further undermined his health during this period. He employed local craftsmen, who worked from rough sketches rather than detailed drawings, and if any detail was less than perfect he demanded its immediate demolition and replacement. Only one real error was made throughout the entire building operation, and this was the attempt to move an old yew tree from the garden at the back of the George and Dragon Inn to the garden of the new house. In March 1930 Griggs moved his printing press into the partly-built house, and the following October the family moved into the completed south wing. Slowly the rest of the building began to take shape around them to form its present U-shaped plan enclosing a small, south-facing garden court. Griggs filled it with simple, sturdy furniture by the best Cotswold craftsmen including, of course, his friends Gimson and the Barnsleys, and Gordon Russell was also to make a contribution. His very first experiment in letter-cutting was carved on the north wing, which read, 'Dover's House was designed and built by Frederick Landseer Maur Griggs'. Apparently, when the house was nearly finished, Griggs invited the workmen to a dinner and invited the BBC to record the occasion. One of the workmen forgot he was on film and began to swear at a colleague, much to the amusement of the daily papers who featured the unfortunate incident in their editions the following morning. After Griggs's untimely death in 1938, Griggs's widow, Nina, continued to live in the house, although she sold it to the artist Sir Frank Brangwyn, who stored his paintings in the south wing during the war. The north wing was destroyed by fire in 1968 but the present owners partly rebuilt and restored the wing with great care during the late 1970s employing Jim Pyment's building firm, and Russell's inscription was salvaged and incorporated at the gable end of the new wing. Although Griggs often referred to the house as 'Griggs Folly', it nevertheless survives as a fitting tribute to the high standards of traditional craftsmanship he sought to perpetuate within the town. Ashbee, himself, was to go so far as to describe the house in a letter to his wife of 1930 as 'one of the loveliest pieces of modern architecture that has been produced in our time'.

Norman Jewson endeavoured to continue Griggs's work of protecting the beauty and character of the town and took over his responsibilities for the Campden Trust. He was to design The Tithe House, opposite the parish church, for the local historian Christopher Whitfield in 1940, and also Porchester Cottage in Westington, built for Will Hart, both of which are competent and sensitive adaptations of the local building style of which Griggs would have wholeheartedly approved.

Other important contributions to the town during this period was the restoration of the Almshouses in 1942 by Guy Pemberton. Pemberton formerly ran an architectural practice in Stratford, but had moved to Chipping Campden in 1927 and collaborated with Griggs on the building of the priest's house in 1935. However he was probably to become best-known in the district for the extraordinary pantomimes he toured around the big houses each year.

Chipping Campden was fortunate to escape the worst effects of the Second World War. The nearest airfield was at Honeybourne down in the Evesham

Whitsuntide procession through the High Street, *c.* 1925.   CT

Vale and only one small war industry was introduced into the town. However sixteen local lives were lost, one of them Griggs's only son John, who was killed at Anzio. Numerous evacuees arrived in the town and, from 1939 until the end of the war, billets were provided in the houses, schools and hotels for the Territorial Army, the Gordon Highlanders and many American servicemen.

Since this time the town has been placed under unceasing threat from modern development, and the enormous increase in traffic now congests its streets and detracts from its outstanding architectural beauty. Yet the thousands of tourists who flock to the town each year also bring in essential income, and so the problem of alleviating the worst effects of the tourist industry presents a seemingly insurmountable challenge to the town's inhabitants and the local planning authorities. However, it is one that must be addressed if the special qualities of the town are to survive. Many retired people have also moved to Campden, and there has arguably been an excess of speculative building that may well be regretted in the future. Despite these modern problems it is remarkable how well the town has retained much of its historic character and traditions during the past century. The memories of Ashbee and his Guild are still strong, fine silverware is still produced at the silk mill, the Cotswold Games thrive once more upon Dover's Hill and the Scuttlebrook Wake fills the streets each Whitsuntide. This sense of history and tradition enriches the lives of all those who visit or live in Chipping Campden and John Masefield was to express the feelings of many local people and visitors to the town in the following lines from his poem 'On Campden':

> On Campden Wold the skylark sings,
> In Campden Town the traveller finds
> The inward peace which beauty brings
> To bless and heal tormented minds.

Let us hope that it will continue to do so for many years to come.

BIBLIOGRAPHY

Ashbee, C.R., *A Book of Cottages and Little Houses*. Batsford, 1906.

——, *Craftsmanship in Competitive Industry*. Essex House Press, 1908.

Baynes, K. and Baynes, K., *Gordon Russell*. Arts Council, 1980.

Beckinsale, R. and Beckinsale, M., *The English Heartland*. Duckworth, 1980.

Carruthers, A. and Johnson, F., *The Guild of Handicraft 1888–1988*. Cheltenham Art Gallery and Museums, 1988.

Crawford, A., Greensted, M. and MacCarthy, F., *C. R. Ashbee and the Guild of Handicraft*. Cheltenham Art Gallery and Museums, 1981.

Crawford, A., *A Tour of Broadway and Chipping Campden*. Victorian Society, 1978.

——, A., (ed.), *By Hammer and Hand*. Birmingham Museums and Art Gallery, 1984.

——, A., *C.R. Ashbee: Architect, Designer and Romantic Socialist*. Yale University Press, 1985.

W. Galsworthy Davies and E. Guy Dawber, *Old Cottages, Farmhouses and Other Stone Buildings of the Cotswold Region*. Batsford, 1905.

Finberg, H.P.R., *The Gloucestershire Landscape*. Hodder & Stoughton, 1975.

Gissing, A., *The Footpath Way in Gloucestershire*. Dent, 1924.

Greensted, M., *The Arts and Crafts Movement in the Cotswolds*. Alan Sutton, 1993.

Horne. J., *Chipping Campden from the Grass Roots*. Evesham, 1982.

Jewson, N., *By Chance I Did Rove*. Roundwood Press, 1983.

MacCarthy, F., *The Simple Life: C.R. Ashbee in the Cotswolds*. Lund Humphries, 1981.

Naylor. G., *The Arts and Crafts Movement*. Studio Vista, 1971.

Powell. G., *The Book of Campden*. Barracuda Books, 1982.

——, 'Frederick Griggs R.A. and Chipping Campden'. Article in *Gloucestershire History*. 1989.

Rushden, P., *The History and Antiquities of Chipping Campden in the County of Gloucestershire*. Privately printed, 1911.

Russell, G., *Designers Trade*. Allen & Unwin, 1968.

Verey, D., *Gloucestershire*, Vol. 2, Buildings of England Series (ed. N. Pevsner). Penguin, 1970.

Walbancke, M., *Annalia Dubrensis*, 1636. Reprinted Scholar Press, 1973.

Whitfield, C., *A History of Chipping Campden*. Shakespeare Head Press, 1958.

Papers in the possession of the Campden and District Historical and Archaeological Society.

INDEX

Page numbers in italic refer to illustrations.

Almshouses 17, *65*, 84, *86*
Arts and Crafts Movement 33–5, 57, 63, 80
Ashbee, Charles Robert viii, 32–6, *35*
 and the Guild of Handicraft 36–47
 involvement in Campden life 49–62
 architectural work in Campden 63–70
 see also 72, 73, 79, 80, 84
Ashbee, Janet 38, 43–4, 52, 59, 61
Atkyns, Sir Robert 26, 27

Barnsley, Ernest and Sidney 46, 57, 63, 84
Bedfont House 26, *26*
Berrington 14, 77, 82
Bradway, William 10
Braithwaite House 37–8, *38*, 57, 60, 68
Brangwyn, Sir Frank 84
Broad Campden 3, 14, 27, 69, 71, 72, 73, 77
Brooklyn 66–7

Calf, Robert 8
Campden House (Hick's mansion) 18–19, *18*, *19*, 21–3, 83
Campden House (Combe House) 15, 31, 60
Campden House, Kensington 17
Campden School of Arts and Crafts 44–5, *44*, *45*, *46*, 73, 79
Campden Railway Station 30–1, *31*, 77
Campden Research Station 77
Campden Society 79
Campden Trust 79, 81–4
Campden, Viscount 60, 74
Campden Wonder 23–4
Catbrook 67–8, *67*, 69, 77, 82
Catholic Church and School 31, 57
Charlcote 26
Clifton House *25*, 26
Coneygree 83
Coomaraswamy, Ananda 60–1, 70
Coomaraswamy, Ethel (Mairet) 60, 62
Cotterell family 26

Daintree 65
Dease, Louis 37, 49, 55
Dickenson, Bob 73
Dover's Court 57, 82–3, *83*
Dover's Games 20–1, *21*, *22*, 42, 86
Dover's Hill 20–1, *20*, 31, 52, 79, 80–1, 86
Dover's House 26, 57, *58*
Downer, Charley 55, 72
Dunn, Martha *53*, 54

Elm Tree House *23*, 25, 37, 44, 63, 68, 69

Essex House Press 37, 40–1, 42, 45, 60
Elsley House *48*, 82

Fels, Joseph 72
Fereby, John and Margery 14, 18
Finberg, H.P.R. 78

Gainsborough, Earl of 13, 19, 37, 54, 60, 65
Gimson, Ernest 46, 57, 63, 84
Gissing, Algernon vii, 38
Grammar School 14, *15*, 16, 17–18, 27, 31, *32*, 37–8, 78, *85*
Green Dragons 26
Grevel, William 9
Grevel's House 9, *9*
Griggs, Frederick Landseer Maur viii, 57, 74–5, 79, 80–5
Guild of Handicraft Ltd viii
 work in Campden 36–47, *40*, *41*, *42*, *47*
 and townspeople 48–55, 59–62, 72
Guild of Handicraft Trust 72
Gybbs, William 10

Harrowby, Earl of 51, 80–1
Hart, George 60, 72
Hart, Will 60, 72, 84
Hicks, Sir Baptist 11, 13, 16–20
High House 65–6
Hulls, Jonathan 27, *29*
Hulls, Richard 8
Huyshe, Reynell 60
Huyshe, Wentworth 60

Island House 37, 49–51, 54, 68, 74
Izod family *54*, 55, 64
Izod Cottage 64–5, *64*

Jewson, Norman 76, 81, 84

Kingcombe 79

Littleworth 77, 82
Loosely, George 56
Lygon Arms, The 80

Mackintosh, Charles Rennie 63, *65*
Mairet, Philippe 61–2
Market Hall *17*, 18, 66, 74, 83
Martin Holland, Rob 36, 42, 66
Martins, The *24*, 26
Masefield, John 44–5, 86
Miller, Alec 38–40, *39*, 57, 69, 72

National Trust, The 73, 81, 83
Noel family 19–20, 31, 83
 see also Gainsborough, Earl of Campden, Viscount
Noel Arms 73
Norman Chapel 3, *3*, 60–1, *61*, 69, 70–1,
North Cotswold Hunt 78, *78*

Old Kings Arms 15, 81, *82*
Old Plough Inn 81–2

Partridge, Fred 38, 60
Payne, Henry 75
Pemberton, Guy 84
Peyton House 15, 26
police station 31, *33*
Porchester Cottage 84
Pyment, Jim *42*, *52*, 54, 72, 84

Ramage, Archie 49–50, 66
Redesdales of Batsford 30, 51, 73
Reeve, Sidney 38
Russell, Sir Gordon 78–9, 84

St James, Church of 1–3, 10–13, *12*, *13*, 52, 73, *81*
silk mill 27, 37, *37*, *40*, 68, 86
Smyth, Thomas 11, 14, 16
Smyth, Anthony 14, 16–17

Thornton, Bill 66, 72
Tithe House, The 84
Town Hall 8, *8*, 74

Volunteer Inn 30, *30*

Weoley, William 4, 10
Westington 6, *6*, 8, 17, 42, *43*, *54*, 57, 69–84
Whiteway settlement 72
Woodroffe, Paul 57, *59*, 70
Woodroffe House 57, 70
Woodward family 25
Woolstaplers Hall 8, 38, *38*, 68–9, *68*
Wright, Frank Lloyd 73